MW01592538

HR Hacks

Tools, tips and templates to get the job done without reinventing the wheel

Lori Kleiman, SPHR SHRM-SCP
ISBN -- 9798650872450
© HR Topics 2020 all rights reserved

Receive copy of all forms and tools electronically by emailing
hacks@hrtopics.com

4th Edition

HR Topics Publishing
Naples, FL
lori@hrtopics.com
www.hrtopics.com
Printed in the United States of America

Acknowledgement

The interaction of people and business have always been fascinating to me and sharing how to make that connection succeed in small businesses has allowed me to create a career of passion and growth. The most successful human resources careers are a culmination of education, experiences, patience, collaboration and study of the human spirit. Combining practical business focus with an emphasis on the human capital that produces results is a winning combination.

As I have travelled through this next phase of my career, I am thankful every day for the shared experiences with others. This book is a compilation of many the HR tools my clients, community and conference attendees have asked for and so it's most appropriate to dedicate this book to you – my audience and my community.

Together we can tackle the best HR Hacks that make human resources accessible for all. I am confident you'll find these hacks helpful and look forward to continuing to learn from you and create ongoing updates available on the book site. Be sure to check it out!

Those that purchased this toolkit directly from HR Topics received a file with all tools and templates are available in Microsoft Word for editing.

If you purchased did not receive the electronic file or purchased through another source,

e-mail hacks@hrtopics.com to receive your file today!

Introduction

Human Resources is critical in all businesses, and the same questions and issues consistently arise. Managers want to know what they don't know, and don't have hours to research answers on the internet. HR Departments of One, and especially those who have HR as part of a larger position in their organization, are constantly searching for HR solutions. Small business owners responsible for HR want to know the same things. And no one wants to be an expert – they just want to know enough to get the job done.

That's exactly why this book was created. Within each chapter you'll find a bit of education, along with forms, tips and tricks and then space to create your own action list. The idea is to give you lots of solutions and ways to use the materials – and then let you get back to work.

The expertise shared in the text comes from a combination of eighteen years of human resource consulting, twelve years of running a family business, and personal interaction with entrepreneurs, human resources professionals, and various executives. HR Topics has compiled a proprietary survey from more than 550 businesses that helps to pull together the human resources puzzle in small business. The survey and practical applications are the baseline for the issues we address in this toolkit.

Top HR issues facing business owners

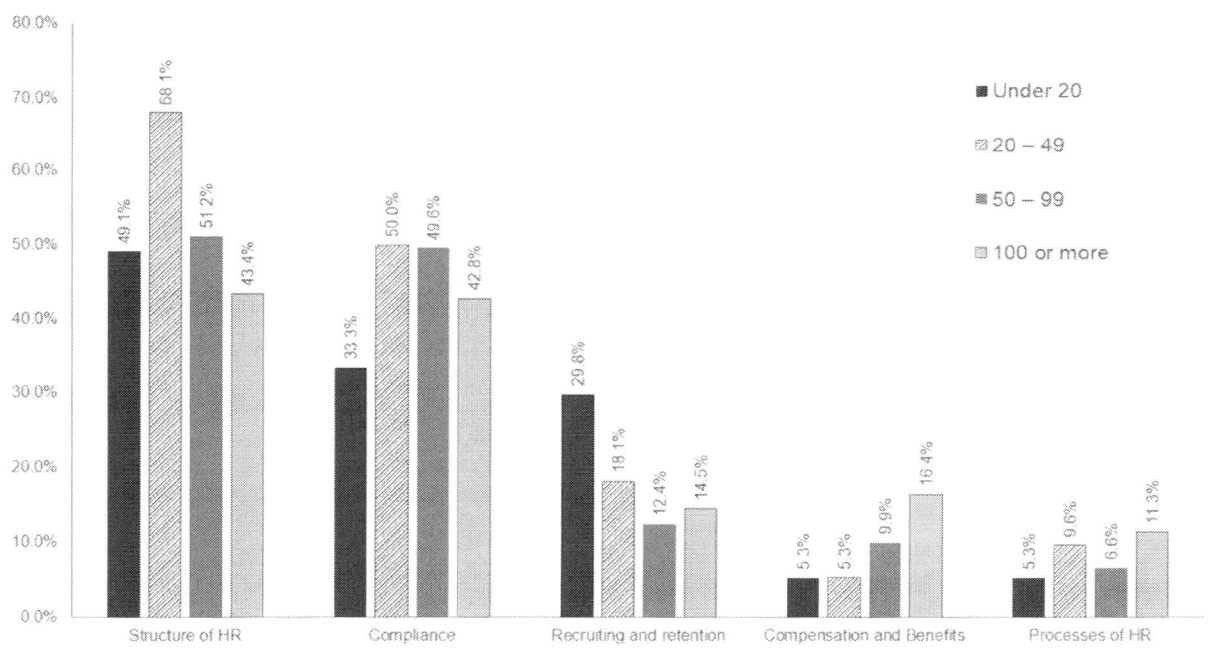

Our survey was compiled by reflecting on the issues raised and the work conducted with business owners and executives in the past twenty years. We continue to gather data and allow the survey to grow as businesses evolve and face new challenges in the twenty first century. The survey has nationwide participation, and includes businesses from various sectors of organizational enterprise including non-profit, manufacturing, professional services, education, construction, and travel. The average business size of survey respondents was 73 employees, with a median number of 176 employees. The difference between the average and the median further highlights the diversity of participation from family businesses and start-ups, as well as publicly traded and larger operations.

The participants are all organizations with operations based in the United States regardless of the ownership structure. Some participants have foreign owners, but the complexity of global human resources is not one we will address here.

My books allow me to connect with HR professionals, small business owners and managers throughout the country. The book titles are:

- Fire HR Now
- HR You Can Use
- Taking your SEAT at the table

In addition, we are now proud to offer HR University. A full platform of HR programs for all levels of HR professionals. Some of our classes include:

- HR 101 and 201
- Test preparation for Human Resource certification
- Mastermind Groups
- A HR membership community

To name a few. Additional details can be found at the back of the book.

Using the feedback from the books, countless workshops and presentations and comments from the weekly blog, this toolkit was created.

TABLE OF CONTENTS

Chapter 1 — Defining Human Resources

Human Resources is relevant to all businesses

All organizations need someone who is focused on the human capital in your business. The question is who it should be and how will you get it done. In this section, we will provide some guidance, so you can determine what is right for your organization in terms of human resources management.

The person watching your human capital should be charged with the responsibility of aligning business goals with employee actions. Studies have proven that high-performing organizations are those that consider recruiting, retention, and development of top talent as a key component of the strategic plan. It doesn't have to be time consuming, just a part of the process.

The first step is to think about the complexity involved with the human capital in your organization. You also want to consider the amount of time your management team is spending on HR activities, rather than running the business areas they have expertise in. I had one client that saw profits rise by bringing in a full-time HR professional to address the time the department managers had to focus on running their various departments.

Share the worksheet on the next page with your leadership team and have a meaningful discussion about HR. Consider the time they are spending on HR, their ability to attract and retain talent, where you want them to be spending time and what they may be hearing from their direct reports.

There are no right answers as to how HR will be visible in the organization based on your situation. However, we believe that by considering these questions as a leadership team, you will be driven to the right solution.

Answering the questions and completing the worksheet on the next page will begin to paint an objective picture of the strengths and opportunities you have in the HR function.

Overall – how critical is it that your employees are retained and engaged in your business operations?

Workforce Planning

What is the typical time it takes to train a new employee in your organization? Complete the chart below to give yourself a good idea of the time and effort involved.

Typical Positions/ Areas	Complexity of skills	Length of time for initial training	Approximate time until new hire is independent	Frequency of turnover	Who is responsible for training	Percentage of workforce in this position
Administration						
Operations						
Customer Service						
Technology						

Do you anticipate a change in your mission in the next 18 months?

Do you anticipate a change in location?

Will your total employee population increase or decrease by 15% in the next 18 months?

Are you involved in an industry or location that tends to be heavily regulated?

Do you consider your payroll and benefit processes to be complex?

CEOs and CFOs do their best to stay on top of employment law and HR processes, but the rules change frequently. Many professionals responsible for human resources have not had formal training, or have the training, but are trying to do it all on their own. Municipalities and industries have specific guidelines that must be addressed. We continually hear that managers simply "don't know what they don't know" in many HR situations. It can take hours of research to find the answer to a situation if you don't have resources.

A great deal of human resources decision making is impacted by case law and precedent handed down in the courts. This makes for a tangled web to navigate when your core competency is based in another area of the business, or you are trying to do it all on your own. At the same time, executives need to be confident that a professional has their back when it comes to human resources.

Check off the statements below that you think reflect your current HR function....

- [ ] Got it covered
- [ ] It's working at a basic level
- [ ] Need more strategic focus
- [ ] All manual administration
- [ ] Have a great HR person
- [ ] HR and Management aligned with goals
- [ ] Great team member handling HR
- [ ] We're on top of best practices
- [ ] Spending excessive fees on legal advice
- [ ] Doing our best and hope it works
- [ ] Looking for training but no idea where to go
- [ ] Not sure what we need to know

Now, look at the pyramid on the next page as a starting place to reflect on all HR needs to accomplish. Consider where your organization is today, who is handling all the pieces shown and whether it's working. Think about whether you have it covered on all levels that you need to drive your business forward.

HR ROLES

STRATEGIC

Leadership Team Member

CULTURE   ETHICS

COMPLIANCE   EXTERNAL RELATIONS

FUNCTIONAL

CANDIDATE SELECTION	NEW HIRE ON-BOARDING	TRAINING AND DEVELOPMENT
PERFORMANCE MANAGEMENT	COMPENSATION AND BENEFITS	PAYROLL	EMPLOYEE ENGAGEMENT

ADMINISTRATIVE

MAINTAIN EMPLOYEE DATA	EMPLOYEE CUSTOMER SERVICE
REPLIES FOR INFORMATION	BENEFIT MANAGEMENT

Adding an HR Team Member

To provide a baseline for comparison, let's review the benchmark ratio of the size of an HR department to total employee population. Current data shows that the average organization has one HR team member for every 133 employees. This ratio is a generalization for all organizations; your appropriate HR needs will change based on factors such as the education, location, technical ability, and fluency of your workforce. The number might also fluctuate based on functions that are outsourced through HR vendors such as benefits, training, and recruiting.

If your organization has less than 133 employees, HR activities cannot be ignored. While HR may not warrant a full-time position in your organization, it is likely taking valuable time away from your leadership team. Organizations that are quite small (under 20 employees) tell us that the main issue surrounding HR is that they just don't know where to begin.

The chart below will help you think about your HR personnel needs as it relates to this benchmark number.

	Indicate a Number or High Medium Low level of importance to your organization
Current number of employees	
Number of employees anticipated to join the organization in next 12 months (*including replacement for those leaving*)	
Level of HR service desired to align with organizational culture	
Employees ability/expectation to be self sufficient	
Use of temporary employees and/or independent contractors	
Needs of employees located outside of main office	
Current use of technology or plan to add technology in the future	
Ability for vendors to support HR (*outsourcing*)	
How do you and your leadership team feel about human capital management today	

Based on the answers above and the benchmark of 1 human resources person for each 133 employees, the right number of hours per week for your organization to spend on HR is....

_____ Hours per week

_____ HR Team Member(s)

There are several ways to engage HR resources that won't break the bank. If you have someone responsible for the HR today, they may need help or access to external resources. If you haven't had an HR focus, there are many options to get started with human resources. We advocate a thorough evaluation of options to determine what is right for your organization including:

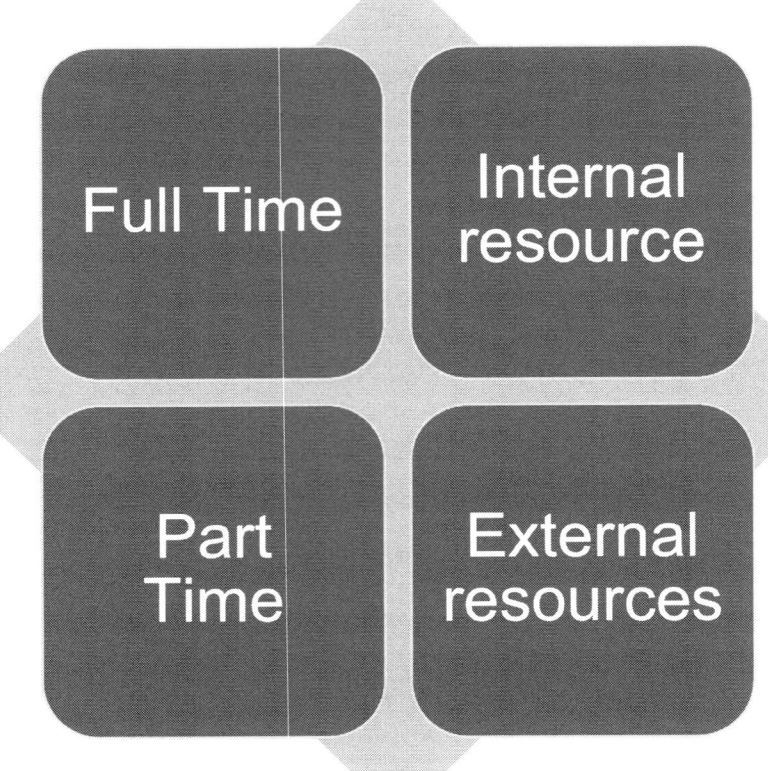

As you see on the chart following this page, our FIPE™ model will help you consider the components, advantages and disadvantages as it relates to your organization. Feel free to mix and match – most organizations use an external resource for benefits, but handle payroll internally for example.

The human resources solution you select will often depend on the ability of your employee population to move through the processes generally associated with the HR function independently. For example, in a manufacturing environment, we may see a full-time HR person brought in earlier to support employees who need help with the technology required for timekeeping and benefit enrollment. Employees in this environment might require more detailed communication through a variety of face-to-face meetings. On the flip side, you may have a virtual workforce that travels throughout the country, autonomously servicing your client base. In that case, employees can be provided online tools so HR needs will be reduced. Other factors that impact the decision to include a dedicated human resources function in your organization are: a high amount of turnover, extensive training, recruiting and retaining top talent, and a higher number of employees for whom English is a second language.

As you review the various worksheets on the following pages, you will create a clear picture of what is right for your team. There is no right or wrong for any organization, and the solutions will ebb and flow as your business, culture and size changes.

The FIPE™ Model

Full-Time	Hiring a full-time resource should be considered for businesses that employ more than 70 employees or those that have administrative needs taxing the current structure of the organization. While 70 employees do not meet the benchmark for a full time professional, it is important to start considering HR as a more formal function at this size. Full-time HR can also be an effective solution in quickly growing organizations or those with exceptional recruiting or training needs. A company that chooses to add this type of HR function to its structure should ensure that their budget is being wisely spent. The management team must expect that the new HR leader will offer fresh ideas that enhance current initiatives, which need a budget! It is incumbent upon current leadership to be open to a new voice. It's not helpful to create a situation in which new ideas of HR management are turned down or when current staff is unwilling to hand over HR responsibilities.
Internal	An internal HR professional will generally mean adding a salary and benefits. However, when considering the budget items that are impacted, there should be a realization that the cost of a professional HR focus can be offset by long term savings. In addition, the expense of HR will be balanced by the ability of your management team to focus time and energy on their areas of expertise. Adding an internal HR professional may mean hiring a new team member. Consider offering the HR position to a current employee. This can be an excellent growth opportunity for a successful team member. The HR position might be offered to develop and add new skills for high performing talent. Selecting a valued member of the team and providing growth and training sends a positive message to the rest of the employees. If co-workers respect the person being moved into the HR role, they will know that management values HR, and appreciates high quality work in current positions.
Part-Time	This is an option for smaller employers, generally those that have fewer than 50 employees. At this size, a dedicated HR professional will struggle to fill 40 hours of impactful work. Part-time HR professionals also work well in organizations with larger employee populations that are geographically dispersed. Employees in remote offices do not expect an immediate reply as they are generally dealing with corporate via phone and email. Your HR function should still be tied to the goals and strategies of the business, bond with employees, and provide the flexibility to ebb and flow as your budget demands. This HR team member should be as skilled and professional as a full-time counterpart.
External	There are several options available to incorporate HR resources utilizing the services of external professionals. Even if you have internal resources, you will find that parts of your human resources puzzle are outsourced. Virtually all organizations outsource the management of their payroll, retirement, and health insurance plans for example. This is an efficient way to utilize talent for their expertise and eliminate the need for your HR resource to be an expert in every aspect of the employee relationship. An external solution can be useful in an organization that is focused on employee engagement as well as those where it is essential for managers to remain focused on critical business functions. The external solution as a replacement to internal focus is also useful in organizations where the reliance on top talent is not a strategic component. In these cases, external groups with a focus on customer service may serve employees well.

© 2020 HR Topics; purchase includes license to use/edit for your organization only.
HR Hacks is not to be construed as legal advice.

Implementing FIPE™ in your organization

Determine what is right for you.... circle the statements that are true for your organization today. Look at what you have indicated and discuss findings with your leadership team. This will enable you to select the right combination of HR resources.

Full time	Internal	Part time	External
70 or more employees	Current employee interested in HR role	Fewer than 100 employees	HR is not a desired focus of the team
Extensive growth next 12 – 18 months	Culture supports strong connection to employees	Plans for HR are less extensive in terms of recruiting, training, and performance management	Concern over compliance without the time/energy to focus on meeting demands
Anticipate high level of recruiting	Management team would benefit from increased reporting and analysis	Anticipated need for HR activities are less than 25 hours per week	Physically dispersed workforce
Extensive training needed for team members	Budget will allow for additional salary and benefits	Employees are comfortable with technology, telephone and email support	Employees comfortable with technology and telephone support
Current person responsible for HR is no longer able or interested in handling HR	Compliance needs to be balanced with organizational plans and culture	Management is interested in information regarding HR, but not ready to invite HR to leadership meetings	Recruiting and training needs are not frequent or complex
Leadership team is open to new ideas and input	Employees are a valued resource	Culture model supports moderate speed in replying to employee and management questions	Administrative functions of payroll and benefits are overwhelming current internal resource
Employees are a valued resource	Culture model supports customer service for employees and managers	Employees are a valued resource	Difficult to attain affordable and competitive benefit program as independent company

Circle the number you had under each column:
Full Time:
Internal:
Part Time:
External:

Based on the number in each category, determine the right mix to serve the needs of your organization. There is no right or wrong, but likely a combination of actions will meet your needs.

Budget Impact of Human Resources

Metrics are the key to effective operational management. In human resources, we utilize metrics to track items that impact productivity and improve the bottom-line profitability of the organization on a regular basis. Consider what line items in your budget and critical components of business needs to be aligned with your human capital. This will help determine whether human resources expertise would be valuable to your organization.

Common indicators that point to additional attention needing to be paid to human resources activities include:

- Expansion plans for the next 12 to 18 months
- Turnover of staff occurring on a regular basis
- Communication from regulatory entities about compliance
- High unemployment rate
- Time spent to identify and attract future talent
- Ability of your management team to meet their goals on a regular basis
- Fragmented policies and procedures throughout the organization
- Budget impact of employee related expenses
- Need to train employees on new processes and technologies
- CFO, Controller or managers saying that it's time to rethink HR

Have conversations with your management team about data they might find useful relating to employees. Reviewing the areas of HR impact with your team will help you determine whether HR needs additional attention in your organization.

The next pages provide tools and templates to consider the impact of HR to your productivity and profitability.

Evaluating How HR Can Impact Your Budget

Consider these items as they impact your organization. Add items at the bottom that may not be represented but still impact your bottom line.

BUDGET LINE ITEM	HR IMPACT
Revenue	• Hire top sales talent • Retention of top sales people • Provide training opportunities to support product needs
Labor Cost	• Understand and minimize overtime • Ability to survey market for competitive pay • Recommend additional hires • Cross-training to reduce overhead
Unemployment	• Proper documentation to support claims • Separate employees when in the interest of business unit • Train managers on real impact of unemployment
Workers compensation	• Safety training and committee • Manage claims • Aggressively assist with return to work
Benefits	• Understand benefits that attract and retain employees • Provide work-life balance benefits that are aligned with employee needs • Contribution strategy management • Administrative functionality • Ensure transparency with payroll to eliminate redundancy
Payroll	• Self-service to eliminate administrative HR activities • Constant review of cost of payroll • Streamline activities to eliminate unnecessary functions
Items specific to your industry	•
Items specific to your region	•
Items specific to your organization	•

Budget Expense Chart

Complete this chart to consider the human capital impact in your organization

Budget Expense	Percentage of total budget or dollars
Labor cost paid – base, overtime and bonus	
Contract labor – all consultants producing work that would have to be hired internally	
Unemployment Expense	
Workers Compensation Insurance	
All benefits – employer contribution only	
Social security and Medicare	
Payroll service fees	
401(k) annual audit and reporting	
Employment attorney fees	
Benefit enrollment platform	
Applicant tracking system	
HR training and conferences	
HR dues and subscriptions	
Employee events – holiday, lunches etc.	
Recruiting expenses	
Training and development of employees	
Other HR activities:	
TOTAL	

HR Metrics

Track these items monthly in your organization to keep an eye on common HR movement. Watch for trends and make changes before they become issues.

	Total Employees (consider full and part time if appropriate)	New Hires	Voluntary Separations (employees that left on their own)	Involuntary Separations (employees that were terminated)	Employees enrolled in benefit plans	Overtime hours worked	Number of open positions at end of month
January							
February							
March							
April							
May							
June							
July							
August							
September							
October							
November							
December							

Use the information you track to determine how human resources can impact your bottom line. Is your current team able to make impactful changes or would a dedicated resource add value by controlling these numbers? Human Resources should be held accountable for meaningful results in these areas.

Anyone can do HR…or NOT!

In small businesses, it's common to find that this mission critical function is given to a team member that has little skill or interest in human resources. It's often the leader of the accounting function. Can you imagine two more different personality types than an HR executive and a chief financial officer? While your accounting leader can and will learn the HR activities, it is rare that it is a part of their job that will be embraced. Taking on ownership of the HR function is one thing, but typically your CFO must spend more time than necessary finding answers to questions and learning the best practices in human resources administration. There are almost always pressing financial issues, and your CFO's time is generally better spent analyzing reports that will drive the business forward rather than walking new hires through initial paperwork.

Many organizations utilize an office manager or administrative manager to handle the HR functions. If time allows, this is often a similar skill set with attention to detail, project management and multi-tasking needs that are common to both positions. Often office managers enjoy the challenge of learning a new skill and field of study that will have long term impact on their career.

Learning the administrative tasks of HR is not the hard part. Finding talent that can embrace the soft skill of being able to work with the line workers and executives at the same time is a critical skill.

Anyone can quickly learn and complete the tasks associated with payroll, benefits and compliance. HR should be the conduit between high level decision making and implementation at the employee level. Therefore, it is critical that you have a team member that will align with your business goals and will convey the desired goals and image desired of the management team.

Your internal resource can have other responsibilities

The HR professional should be a trusted member of the team. It is critical that HR be aligned with the leadership team for the employee management portion of their job. They need to understand where the business is headed and what challenges lie ahead. Only with this information will they be able to recruit and develop talent to support the organization of the future.

The team member your employees view as their contact must be able to explain and support leadership decisions and policy. Allow the team member you select to have access to the strategic information and basis for leadership decisions. This will allow HR to be a trusted resource for employees and provide a connection with the organization that is so important to employees.

On the page that follows you will find a basic HR job description. This is a high-level overview of typical HR activities. There are also some suggestions included for background of an HR team member. You should create a customized document that is appropriate for your organization. A blank template can be found on the website, as well as in the recruiting section of this book.

Staying on top of ever-changing compliance requirements

Ideally, an annual training budget for a team member charged with HR responsibility should be in the range of $1,500 to $3,000 annually. Depending on your location, a budget for travel may be required as well. This would allow the novice HR administrator to attend a few entry level programs, and your more experienced HR professional to attend one or two annual conferences to stay on top of industry best practices. If that seems out of reach, there are generally programs conducted by employment law firms in your area at no charge that should be attended annually.

If you choose to leave HR with one or more department managers, this budget is still appropriate. Your CFO or office manager will need to attend HR specific compliance training each year at a minimum.

JOB DESCRIPTION – HR Team Member

This is a sample job description for HR. Depending on your organization, the essential functions will change

Job Title:	HR Team Member	Department:	
Education Anticipated:	Consider HR certification as a requirement. This will provide confidence in the knowledge as well as a commitment to the profession. The four common designations are: PHR, SPHR, SHRM-CP or SHRM-SCP. In California, there is a CA designation as well.		

OVERVIEW:

Member of leadership team to direct and impact the human capital of the organization. Creates a positive culture and supports strategic goals

ESSENTIAL FUNCTIONS OF THE POSITION:

- Provide management with information or training related to interviewing, performance appraisals, counseling techniques, and documentation of performance issues.
- Maintain current knowledge of applicable employment law appropriate for organization.
- Analyze employment-related data, prepare reports and make recommendations.
- Confer with management to develop or implement policies and procedures.
- Manage full cycle recruiting program.
- Conduct new employee orientations.
- Provide customer service to employees.
- Manage employee data base with updated information as appropriate.
- Maintain and update human resources documents, such as organizational charts, employee handbooks, or performance alignment process.
- Management of vendors and interaction with service providers.
- Assist with or manage payroll.
- All other duties as requested by management.

QUALIFICATIONS AND EDUCATION REQUIREMENTS:

Strong communication and administrative skills. Attention to detail as well as the ability to work well with multiple levels of employees in the organization. College degree or equivalent experience preferred.

DESIRED COMPETENCIES:

- Communication skills
- Detail oriented
- Research and monitoring
- Judgment and decision making
- Active learning

PREFERRED SKILLS:

Intermediate level or higher in Microsoft Office products. Use of previous payroll or HRIS program including report writing and data management. Comfortable speaking and presenting before large groups of employees. Ability to speak additional language if appropriate.

PHYSICAL REQUIREMENTS:

Employee will typically sit for long periods of time. Must be able to use hands to operate computer and file extensive paperwork. Ability to communicate with employees and candidates for employment.

HR leaders need to possess exceptional skills as a:

Communicator

ability to present complex issues to management
work with line employees who have a wide diversity of skills
support employees for whom English is a second language

Trusted Advisor

able to coach and guide the leadership team in various situations
understand the subtlety necessary in areas of compliance

Executive

participate as member of the united team driving business forward
interact with all areas of business
professional experience in overall business

Business Leader

possess knowledge of the entire business including:
budget
technology
finance
sales
operations

Innovator

provide solutions to problems
evolve through new services, programs, and policies
think outside the box
ask questions that go beyond the norm

Relationship Manager

ability to set expectations
evaluate performance
negotiate terms
engage services

Action Items for how HR will look in your organization:

1.	**Review the current HR administration with your leadership team**
a.	**Create a list of the HR tasks you need in your organization**
b.	**Complete and discuss FIPE™ worksheet with your leaders**
c.	**Ask managers for HR activities they are completing and the time spent each week**
2.	**Get input from trusted advisors – do they feel you would benefit from an HR resource**
3.	**Review your budget for a reliance on HR activities**
4.	**Customize the HR job description. Determine the required hours needed**
5.	**Consider internal candidates that may be interested in taking on HR responsibilities**

Chapter 2 — Compliance

Businesses of all sizes have government regulations they must be aware of and comply with. This includes the smallest business with only one employee on a part-time basis. That employee is still entitled to proper pay and a work environment that is free of discrimination.

Human resources professionals consider compliance a major part of their function. In businesses that do not have a formal HR function, compliance awareness should be assigned to a member of the management team. The organization must keep current with laws and understand which of those impacts the organization. There are deadlines throughout the year that stem from many of these laws and dictate when forms must be completed and where to report employment statistics. Typically, states, cities, counties, and other municipalities create additional regulations addressing more stringent requirements that must be complied with as well.

Organizations that operate facilities in multiple locations are required to comply with regulations specific to where employees work, which gets especially complicated when a business operates across state lines. Add to that the fact that much of what HR considers when making decisions are not on-the-book regulations, but ever evolving legal precedence. The verdict in a lawsuit will guide HR professionals in the application of policies and procedures to ensure your organization will not end up with a similar legal action. Since a business cannot control which employees will pursue legal action HR professionals can learn from the example of others and protect the company when possible.

But don't be mistaken: while HR is responsible for awareness of and compliance with laws, it should not be the primary focus of your HR function. Laws must be adhered to, but they are also a springboard for critical business conversations. It is not productive to have an HR function that spends time using legal compliance as the excuse to keep an organization from meeting strategic goals. There are many ways to simultaneously address business needs, remain compliant, and move initiatives forward. Having a strategic HR partner is essential to ensure that your managers are receiving informed counseling on legal obligations, as well as brainstorming solutions that meet the needs of the operation at the same time.

Ultimately, compliance is the responsibility of the entire management team and should be the concern of ownership. The fines levied by the Department of Labor, Equal Employment Opportunity Commission, Department of Homeland Security, Occupational Safety and Health Administration and the Internal Revenue Service can be staggering. The highest fines are those that are given to employers who act in a willful disregard of requirements. Those are the business owners, executives, and human resources professionals that were aware laws and protocols existed but did nothing to address the compliance requirements at their organization.

How do I know what impacts my organization?

Many business owners and HR administrators are not in tune with the full scope of employment law that impacts their organization. Consider your knowledge of the list below which are the laws that typically impact every business:

- Title VII of Civil Rights Act
- American with Disability Act
- Family and Medical Leave Act
- Fair Labor Standards Act
- Immigration Reform and Control
- Federal Labor Relations Act/Board
- Occupational Safety and Health Administration

These are the major laws HR deals with on a consistent basis. The complexity of managing compliance starts with an understanding of which laws impact your organization, what reporting requirements are involved, and how to apply each to your employees.

On the following pages, you will find an overview of major employment laws that impact most businesses. We provide links to the government web sites which will allow you to have the most current, up to date information.

CRITICAL NOTE: This is a chart of FEDERAL law only and is not exhaustive. Each state, city and municipality will have additional laws you are obligated to comply with. Stay connected to local sources who can provide critical updates on this information such as your State Department of Labor and local attorneys specializing in employment law.

If your organization has a contract with one or more unions, you may find some variance based on your negotiations. Always defer to your contract and/or labor counsel.

This list is representative of the laws that are addressed by many small businesses. Additional laws may apply based on location, industry, and status as a government contractor. It is not intended to be a comprehensive list. As with all information, check with your legal counsel for additional information or compliance.

Compliance Chart

Fewer than 15 employees must be aware of:

	Overview	To be aware of:	Website for additional guidance
Fair Labor Standards Act	Establishes minimum wage, overtime pay, record keeping, and child employment standards impacting employees. Some industries such as religious organizations may be exempt.	Rules relating to who is entitled to overtime. Pay can be very complex for travel and waiting periods. Comp time is never allowed in private business. Meal and break laws will be defined by each state and must be checked.	https://www.dol.gov/agencies/whd/flsa
Immigration Reform and Control Act	Requires employers to collect information regarding an employee's identity and employment eligibility and document that information on Form I-9. Must use form that is currently in effect.	Form must be completed within 72 hours of employee starting work. Your only obligation is to complete the form, but many employers choose to retain copies of the documents provided.	https://www.uscis.gov/i-9
Equal Pay Act	Prohibits sex-based wage discrimination between men and women in the same establishment who perform jobs that require substantially equal skill, effort, and responsibility under similar working conditions.	Some exceptions exist such as a seniority or merit system, difference in quantity of work, and geography.	http://www.eeoc.gov/laws/statutes/epa.cfm
Occupational Safety and Health Administration	Sets standards and conducts inspections to ensure that employers are providing safe and healthful workplaces.	Requirements include maintaining a log of injury/illness, annually posting summary of the log, and investigating workplace accidents.	https://www.osha.gov/recordkeeping/index.html
Fair Credit Reporting Act	Protects the privacy of consumer report information and guarantees the information supplied by consumer reporting agencies is as accurate as possible. Sets forth legal obligations of employers who use consumer reports. Requires specific authorization by candidates or employees.	Many states have laws which prohibit or limit an employer's use of consumer credit reports or criminal records checks and/or prohibit discrimination based on credit or criminal history information. Be sure to check the applicable laws in your state and consult with an employment law attorney who knows your state laws to ensure full compliance.	It's most critical that you check state law. Be especially aware of the "Ban the Box" laws that do not allow you to ask about conviction at time of application.

Google: State followed by background check for example |

15 and more employees (above plus...)

	Overview	To be aware of:	Website for additional guidance
Title VII of Civil Rights Act; and its amendment in 1991	Prohibits employment discrimination based on race, color, religion, sex and national origin or other protected class or characteristic. Also, prohibits harassment in the workplace. The amendment set maximum recovery penalties.	State and municipalities have broadened the scope in their areas. Be sure to check local law. Better yet, just treat all employees fairly! Similar protection exists for small employers based on state law.	http://www.eeoc.gov/ Many tools relating to Discrimination in the work place. Search on Title VII and more
Americans with Disabilities Act	Prohibits employment discrimination against qualified individuals with disabilities. Requires that employers reasonably accommodate the known physical or mental limitations of an otherwise qualified individual with a disability who is an applicant or employee, unless doing so would impose an undue hardship on the operation of the employer's business.	Job descriptions should clearly define the essential functions and the physical requirements of the job. Understand the concept of a reasonable accommodation and speak with an attorney prior to separating any employee with a disability. Always engage in conversations with employees about their requests for accommodations.	http://www.ada.gov/
Genetic Information Notification Act	Prohibits discrimination against applicants, employees, and former employees based on genetic information relating to individual or family member.	GINA notification has been added to required employment posters. Ensure your poster is up to date. You can download a free poster at the web site shown.	https://www.dol.gov/sites/default/files/ebsa/about-ebsa/our-activities/resource-center/fact-sheets/gina.pdf

20 or more employees (all of above, plus...)

	Overview	To be aware of:	Website for additional guidance
COBRA	Provides most members of employer sponsored health insurance the right to choose to continue group health benefits for limited periods of time if they lose their health benefits. Employee pays full cost of insurance plus administrative fee.	The paperwork requirements are very specific and it is generally advisable to have your benefit broker or health plan provide this service. If under 20 employees check state law.	https://www.dol.gov/sites/default/files/ebsa/about-ebsa/our-activities/resource-center/publications/an-employers-guide-to-group-health-continuation-coverage-under-cobra.pdf
Age Discrimination in Employment Act	Prohibits employment discrimination against persons 40 years of age or older.	Upon separation, specific documents must be given if providing severance. Check with your attorney before creating a separation agreement.	https://www.eeoc.gov/laws/statutes/adea.cfm

50 or more employees (All of above, plus...)

	Overview	To be aware of:	Website for additional guidance
Family and Medical Leave Act	Entitles eligible employees to take unpaid, job-protected leave for up to twelve weeks per year if specified family and medical reasons are met. There are provisions regarding paid time off, definition of the year, benefits while on leave etc. FMLA also covers leave for family members of active military in certain situations. Note: An employee must work at a location where the company employs 50 or more employees within 75 miles and meet certain other requirements with respect to time worked.	Specific forms should be completed by the medical professional as well as the employer. All forms can be found on the government website. If employee is not able to return after 12 weeks, ADA must be considered before terminating the employee. The twelve weeks of leave does not need to be consecutive or paid.	https://www.dol.gov/agencies/whd/fmla

Need help mastering HR terms?

We've got an app for that!

Download the HR Cards app from iTunes or Google Play

It's a fun and easy way to learn over 1200 HR terms!

Calendar of Critical Dates

JANUARY	✓ Prepare OSHA 300 A ✓ Gather Data for 5500 reporting ✓ Advise employees of increase allowed in retirement and flex spending accounts if allowed by law ✓ Send W2s and 1099s as appropriate ✓ Be sure to change benefit deductions in payroll ✓ Download new W4 with current year for new hires
FEBRUARY	✓ February 1st – Post OSHA 300A log ✓ Consider total compensation statements for previous year
MARCH	✓ March 1st – Medicare Part D reporting due ✓ First Friday – National Employee Appreciation day ✓ EEO-1 (over 100 employees) and VETS 4212 (federal contractors) reports due
APRIL	✓ April 1st – H-1B filing begins ✓ April 30th – Take down OSHA 300A and retain for 5 years
JULY	✓ File 5500 for Retirement plan and other benefits if required
AUGUST	✓ Send Summary Plan Description of retirement plan if required
SEPTEMBER	✓ Consider your holiday schedule for payroll and time off and publish to employees
OCTOBER	✓ Medicare Part D credible coverage notices to employees ✓ October 16 – National Boss' Day
NOVEMBER	✓ Receipt of unemployment rate – verify accuracy
DECEMBER	✓ Calculate imputed income for life, personal use of auto, etc. ✓ Subchapter S corps: Calculate tax implications and reimburse accordingly
ANNUALLY	✓ Review employee handbook for necessary updates ✓ Determine if your current employment posters are up to date ✓ Remove all I-9's for terminated employees that are no longer required ✓ Communicate with employees regarding lack of tolerance for harassment and discrimination ✓ Complete HR Audit provided as part of HR Hacks

Each organization will have specific deadlines based on size, industry and location. This is not all inclusive or to be taken as legal advice.

Assessing Your Current HR Operation

You need to trust that your management team and HR professional are doing the job, but at the same time verification is essential. Just as you audit accounting on a regular basis, audit your HR function. The stakes are too high to just assume everything is in compliance.

The audit can be as specific or comprehensive as you need to feel comfortable. You can complete an audit yourself or hire outside professionals to handle the audit. On the pages that follow, we provide a standard HR Audit checklist. Often organizations and HR professionals use this as an exercise to benchmark against best practices and determine if processes have slipped. Use this as a tool to identify where you are in compliance and where there are opportunities for improvement.

There are multiple options when considering external professionals to conduct the assessment. Labor attorneys and human resources consultants typically offer this service. You can also find resources by inquiring with your payroll and employee benefit vendors. If you do choose to work with an employment attorney to conduct your assessment, ensure that they are a legal expert that spends most of their time in employment matters. A general corporate attorney who advises you on employee issues may conduct the audit, but generally doesn't have the depth of knowledge of human resources to give practical advice or solutions. If compliance were your only goal, an employment attorney would be a valuable resource. An effort should be made to engage an attorney who has a focus on compliance as well as expertise in best practices. Ask if they can offer the service as part of an annual agreement or at a fee that is within your organization's budget.

HR consultants are an excellent resource for assessments. They provide the expertise in both compliance and best practices. You should look for a consultant that is certified by either HRCI or SHRM. The SPHR and SHRM-SCP designation indicates that they have passed a stringent exam on the strategic and compliance components of the HR function, as well as having met the annual continuing education requirements for designation.

Considerations for various auditing options

Internal resources	External resources
Can be time consuming	Can be expensive
May not have depth of knowledge needed	Not aligned with the culture
Difficult to audit own work	May have standards that don't apply
Less expensive	Will understand full scope of work
Understands the culture of the organization	Possibly provide "cookie-cutter" solutions

What will I end up with?

Regardless of internal or external auditors, the deliverable from your audit should include a complete review of compliance as well as suggestions for best practices of your human resources function. A productive process will end with suggestions for change based on urgent impact to the organization. All suggestions should come complete with action to be taken, deadline and cost for completion.

How often do we need to do this?

The idea of the assessment is to identify process issues or ensure compliance with legal changes. For this reason, annual review is recommended. Changes in employment laws are relatively frequent. Consequently, it is important that employers be kept informed of changes in the law, as well as any changes in best practices and other guidelines for human resources management. If time or resources are limited, select the areas of greatest concern and impact to your organization and review those on a regular basis.

Want to stay connected with additional tools, live time with Lori and access to great conversation? Join our community!

Email hacks@hrtopics.com for details!

HR Assessment

Recruiting

- [ ] Job Descriptions
  - One for each position
  - Accurately reflect essential functions of position
  - List valid job-related qualifications
  - Define the physical requirements for the job
  - Signed by employee
- [ ] Employment Application
  - Asks for information relevant to the position only
  - Does not ask about citizenship – only ability to work in US
  - Use care when asking for arrest record – see state law called Ban the Box
  - Education does not ask for date of graduation
  - Candidates to sign off on an agreement including:
    - All information provided is true
    - Employment will be offered on an at-will basis
    - Agree to comply with policies including drug testing
    - Authorization to check background and references
    - Application only valid for 30 days
- [ ] Job positing
  - Discriminatory language is not used
  - Qualifications are appropriate for position
- [ ] Reference Checking
  - Is there a formal practice in place
  - Candidates sign authorization
  - FCRA documents provided

- [ ] Offer Letter
  - Salary should be stated in "per pay-period" amount
  - No promise of future benefits
  - Employment-at-will language
  - Date must be returned or offer will be rescinded
  - Consider if confidentiality or non-compete agreements should supplement the offer letter
  - Signature of candidate

New Employee Procedures & Paperwork

- [ ] I-9 Completion; if E-verify is used check compliance
- [ ] Employee's Withholding Allowance Certificate (W-4) for year of hire; state and federal
- [ ] Direct deposit authorization
- [ ] New Hire Reporting requirements for state
- [ ] Employee Handbook evidence of receipt
- [ ] Utilization of new hire checklist
- [ ] Signature of arbitration and waiver of class action
- [ ] Receipt of company property with value
- [ ] Confidentiality and Non-disclosure agreements
- [ ] Review any other forms provided for completion and non-discrimination

Employee Handbook

- [ ] Provided to all employees; describe online access
- [ ] Overall language provides for flexibility by management
- [ ] Contains essential policies including:
  - At-will employment
  - Pay practices
  - Equal opportunities
  - Anti-harassment and discrimination
  - Internet and email policies
  - Confidentiality
  - FMLA if you have over 50 employees within 75 miles

See employee handbook checklist on page 40

I-9 Audit

- [ ] I-9 in active file for all current employees
- [ ] Retained in location other than employee file
- [ ] All employees completed within 72 hours of hire
- [ ] Utilizing proper form for date of hire
- [ ] Section 2 properly completed
- [ ] Section 3 signed by company representative
- [ ] Retain only those required for terminated employees
  - The later of 3 years from date of hire or 1 year following date of termination

See I-9 audit document on next page

Compensation

- ☐ Evaluation of compensation for those in similar positions
- ☐ Recordkeeping of work hours
  - Complete
  - True reflection of work
  - Signed by employee
- ☐ Paid time off categories tracked and enforced
- ☐ All appropriate withholdings occur
  - FICA
  - State and federal taxes
  - Imputed income as appropriate
  - Overtime paid on 40 hours each week
- ☐ Classification of exempt and non-exempt employees is accurate
- ☐ Overtime law properly followed
- ☐ Independent contractors are properly classified

  These topics are further discussed in the compensation section

Benefits

- ☐ All ERISA, HIPAA and COBRA communication provided
- ☐ Employees enrolled or signed waiver of benefits
- ☐ COBRA provided if applicable; under 20 employees review state law
- ☐ FMLA documents provided properly if over 50 employees
- ☐ 5500 completed for insurance plans and submitted annually
- ☐ Imputed income properly calculated

Employee Files

- ☐ One official file for each employee
- ☐ Files kept in locked cabinet/office
- ☐ Virtual files password protected
- ☐ Medical information retained in separate files
- ☐ Performance reviews exist and signed/dated by both employee and manager
- ☐ All new hire paperwork complete and signed
- ☐ Policy established on employees viewing/copying file per state law
- ☐ Retention policy established for terminated employees
- ☐ Ensure that unnecessary documents are not filed

Recordkeeping/Documentation

- ☐ Federal and state employment posters
  - If more than 20% of workforce speaks another language, posters in that language
- ☐ Employees sign performance documentation
- ☐ EEO-1 filed annually if over 100 employees
- ☐ Document retention and destruction policy

Training and Development

- ☐ Are managers trained on compliance issues relating to HR:
  - Overtime Law
  - Proper interview techniques
  - Process for termination
  - ADA/FMLA/Work Comp
  - Reporting of absence more than 3 days
  - Harassment and discrimination
  - Internet/computer policies
  - Retaliation compliance
- ☐ Anti-harassment training conducted annually for all employees
- ☐ Hazardous materials training as appropriate
- ☐ Retain attendance sheets for all training

Employee Discipline/Termination

- ☐ Discipline policy established and maintained
- ☐ Procedure for investigation of employee incidents and complaints
- ☐ Approval for references in future
- ☐ Process for termination established
  - Who approves the termination
  - Notification to others as appropriate
  - Retrieval of company property
  - Eliminate access to all company resources
  - Final pay
  - Benefit termination and notification

Safety

- ☐ OSHA 300 log retained for 5 years
- ☐ OSHA 300A posted annually
- ☐ Hazardous material training provided
- ☐ Lockout/tag out training provided

Conducting an I-9 Audit

Each year it is recommended that you review your I-9 documentation and correct any errors. While the obligation under the law is to complete them accurately the first time, the Department of Homeland Security has looked favorably upon businesses that are trying to ensure compliance.

1.   Print a list of current employees from payroll in alphabetical order

2.   Gather all I-9's and sort in alphabetical order

3.   Start with your payroll list. For each person currently employed, verify:

    1.   Employee has completed each portion of section one.

    2.   Employee has signed and dated the document in section one.

    3.   The organization has completed the documentation viewed in Column A OR both Column B and C. It is not acceptable to just attach the documents, each line in these columns must be completed.

    4.   Section 2 – ensure the date of hire has been written in. Someone from the organization must also sign and date the form. The company address must be filled in. It is acceptable to use a stamp for the address.

4.   If you have an I-9 for an employee who is no longer employed, remove it from your I-9s. Determine if you need to retain the document. I-9s must be retained for former employees for a period of time. To determine if the form is required consider the requirement:

Required: One I-9 for each employee plus separated employees for the longer of 3 years from date of hire or 1 year from date of termination, whichever is longer.

Complete this worksheet if unsure:

Separated Employee date of hire: _____   3 years from that date: _____

Separated Employee date of separation: _____   1 year from that date: _____

Which of the two dates is most in the future: _____

This is the date beyond which you no longer need to retain the I-9.

<u>Correcting mistakes that you find</u>: Likely you will find mistakes. Make those changes directly on the I-9 document in a color pen other than the original completion. Initial and date any changes that you make. Create a "note to file" of all errors found and correction made and put that in the front of your I-9 binder so you have a permanent record of changes.

Documentation Requirements in Human Resources

Documentation is essential in the HR function, and must be properly managed. When there is any dispute with an employee, the first thing reviewed is the written record.

Law requires a great deal of documentation relating to the lifecycle of employees and the organization as an overall entity. Examples include:

- I-9 form
- OSHA 300 and 300A log
- FMLA paperwork
- COBRA forms
- EEO-1 annual report

and many others documents which are often dependent on your size and industry.

Forms issued by government offices change often but are updated and available on the Internet. Be sure to watch for updates. If you join our private membership community you'll be the first to know! Email us at hacks@hrtopics.com for details!

There are many documents used within the HR function that are not required by law. However, if they are utilized in your organization the compliance impact should be considered. The forms in this category include:

- employment application
- performance review forms
- written warnings
- all other notes and documents kept relating to the employee and the workplace

Without documentation, a game of "he said, she said" develops and rarely is this resolved satisfactorily.

Keeping records on employment decisions is a critical step in compliance. There should always be a formal record to indicate communication with employees has occurred around a given workplace incident. This will be used if there is a dispute with unemployment, a discrimination claim, or charge of wrongful termination. At the same time, not every conversation has to have a formal notice signed by the employee put into a file. There are times when a verbal warning is appropriate, or a manager can make note of a conversation without the employee's signature. Make this decision based on the severity and frequency of the situation. This is further discussed in chapter 5 relating to employee performance.

It is critical to maintain documentation that is consistent among employees. In many employment disputes, the first thing courts or government entities review is how other similarly situated employees were treated. For this reason, we suggest that a single individual be responsible for the human resources function rather than each department manager being allowed to handle and document employment situations.

Employee File Maintenance

All organizations should maintain official employee files. In the best case, these are maintained by a trusted member of your team and kept locked in a central location. In many cases, there are documents that should be part of employee files which are currently retained in various areas of the organization. Finance keeps what they need related to payroll; the office manager retains portions related to emergency contact and key card access, and the department manager has information concerning performance and training. Files that are strewn all over the organization can be difficult to access and will rarely meet the compliance obligations of the organization. Maintaining a central file system allows the organization to ensure that all pieces of the compliance puzzle are maintained.

Employee files may be maintained electronically. This provides a central storage and will typically attach to your payroll system for security and ease of retrieval. Virtual files are acceptable under compliance requirements, and an excellent use of technology. With proper security, the virtual files will enhance productivity and accessibility of employee information by your management team.

In almost all jurisdictions employees must be allowed to access the files that are retained relating to their employment. However, that does not mean employees can approach you at any time demanding that you to drop everything and provide access. The exact timeframe is based on state law. You should be familiar with the obligations of your state and use the time allotted to ensure the file is complete and you are comfortable with the contents prior to providing an employee access. Many states will allow you to charge employees for any copies that are requested. While it is not recommended for current employees, it can be an effective deterrent and cost containment process for former employees or their authorized representatives.

The next page provides guidelines for maintaining employee files.

TO BE RETAINED IN AN EMPLOYEE FILE

Each organization will have various documents in the employment relationship. You may not have all these forms, and you may have some that are not listed. Include what is appropriate for your organization. These may be retained today in electronic files that are password protected.

- **Job description** for the position
- **Application** for all employees and resume if provided
- Documentation of **reference check**
    - If background or credit checks were completed, retained in a separate location
- **Offer** of employment
- IRS Form **W-4** for the year of hire and applicable state forms
- If employee will be driving, copy of **driver's license** and approval to verify annually
- Signed **acknowledgment** of employee handbook
- **Orientation checklist** signed by employee
- **Performance evaluations** including disciplinary actions taken
    - Dated and signed by company and employee
    - Verbal **warnings** noted as such
    - Documentation indicating salary or position changes
- Employee **benefit forms**
    - Should not contain medical information – if medical information is required, retain document in separate location
- **Emergency contacts**
- Completion of **training programs**
- Proof of any **certifications** attained
- **Contract**, written **agreement**, receipt, or acknowledgment between the employee and the employer for example:
    - Non-compete agreement
    - Confidentiality agreement
    - Employment contract
    - Agreement relating to a company-provided car
- **Separation information**
    - Voluntary – written resignation from employee
    - Involuntary – process and documentation used by company to arrive at decision

It is not necessary to keep a copy of every correspondence relating to an employee such as verifications of employment, change of address and updated phone number. The purpose of the file is to retain relevant information to document the relationship between the employee and the organization.

Employee Handbooks

Policies can both help and hinder an organization. Once policies are documented, the organization will be obligated to follow the procedures outlined and benefits specified. Some owners feel that having an employee handbook will take away their flexibility to make changes for the organization. This is not always the case. A well written employee handbook is a roadmap that provides your team with guidelines by which to operate. The handbook ensures that all department managers treat their employees the same way and gives confidence to leadership that the culture of the organization is being maintained through policy.

Create policies that leave enough flexibility for situational decision making in the future. It is essential to use terms such as "generally" "often" and "may" rather than more concrete terms such as "will" "always" and "required." There are situations that arise in the employment relationship that require rules to be "bent" for the circumstances. This should be the exception, but when modification is given to an employee for a valid business reason, it is certainly acceptable. Your handbook makes certain that decisions made regarding employees' questions and requests are based on objective criteria.

There are many policies that are essential to every employee handbook. Among the most critical policies to include are:

- At-will employment
- Anti-harassment and discrimination
- Computer systems, social media and email use
- Pay practices
- Confidentiality of company property, medical information and employee data

There are many thoughts on creating an employee handbook. Some managers want to document everything and include processes and procedures for all business interactions. Others feel that having a handbook will limit their ability to be flexible and make changes to the employment relationship as the needs change. We recommend somewhere in the middle.

The handbook should not include processes, forms or other "how to" steps. The idea of the employee handbook is to paint a picture of the employment relationship as it exists for all. You should have a handbook to provide guidelines to new hires and ensure that all managers are operating under the same principals. At the same time – the language must be flexible enough to provide decision making at a given point in time.

If you currently have a handbook, use the checklist on the next page as a guide to see what might be missing and what could be improved. Your handbook should be reviewed by your leadership team annually to ensure the stated topics are still appropriate for your operations. Consider legal review as well to verify compliance.

If you do not have a handbook, we recommend a handbook writing software or working with an attorney or HR consultant to develop one. Once created, the handbook tone should reflect the culture of your organization.

The handbook should be reviewed annually to ensure consistency and an accurate reflection of current policy and process. It is easier to change and adapt your handbook as you expand, rather than start a handbook when you have 50 employees and multiple operating rules within various departments.

The policies and checklist on the pages that follow are a good starting point to ensure your current handbook is complete, or provide a starting point to begin the creation of policies that will become your handbook as you grow.

Employee Handbook Checklist

We have identified the typical sections of a handbook and what we would expect them to include. It is not productive to have an enormous handbook that includes every policy and procedure. For example, we do not recommend a travel reimbursement section if your organization only has a few people that travel for company business. Those policies can be provided to the appropriate individuals.

This is not an exhaustive list, or a suggestion that everything must be included. This list is intended for review of a current handbook quickly to determine if updates are required.

Welcome Information

☐ Warm welcome from executive, HR or ownership
- Be sure this language does not compromise employment at will

☐ Mission and value of the organization if available

☐ Equal Opportunity Employment and non-discrimination

☐ Employment-at-will restated – it should also appear on the front cover

☐ If multiple states, be clear which state law you are basing the handbook on. Indicate that state and local law will always supersede.

☐ Ethics expectations

Employment Information

☐ Anti-harassment and discrimination policy

☐ American with Disability Act policy

☐ Retention of employee files

☐ Office equipment

☐ Hours of work

☐ Attendance and punctuality

☐ Dress code

☐ Code of conduct

☐ Performance management

☐ GINA notification

☐ Workers compensation benefit

Compensation and Benefits

☐ Payroll Practices
- Define a work week including day and time the week begins and ends
- Overtime pay
- Maintenance of timekeeping records
- Direct Deposit
  - Check state law to determine if mandatory direct deposit is acceptable
- Payroll check date

☐ Can checks be picked up early if on vacation?

☐ Error in payroll calculation statement

☐ General explanation of insurance programs
- Do not be specific, these tend to change

☐ Paid time off benefits
- Vacation/Sick/Personal
- Bereavement
- Jury Duty
- Holidays
- Witness and voting time off can be considered depending on state law

☐ COBRA availability

☐ Requirement to report accident within 72 hours

☐ Family and Medical Leave if over 50 employees in 75 miles

General Policies

- [ ] Internet use
- [ ] Privacy of emails and web sites
- [ ] Social Media expectations
- [ ] Drug and alcohol use
- [ ] Smoking in the workplace
- [ ] Recording and video
- [ ] Bring Your Own Device
- [ ] Arbitration
- [ ] Statement not to infringe on rights under Title 7 of NLRB (ability to speak to each other about pay)

Review State Law for

- [ ] Meal and break requirements
- [ ] Paid time off obligations
- [ ] Jury Duty
- [ ] Sick leave
- [ ] Voting
- [ ] Domestic Violence
- [ ] Crime Victim
- [ ] Organ Donor
- [ ] Marijuana rights and requirements
- [ ] Minimum wage
- [ ] Gender disclosure
- [ ] Obligations of training on Anti-harassment

Policies that are not essential, but often considered by organizations

- [ ] Nepotism
- [ ] Solicitation of materials and use of bulletin board
- [ ] Romance/dating in the workplace
- [ ] Violence in the workplace
- [ ] Internal investigations and searches
- [ ] Tuition reimbursement
- [ ] Concealed carry weapons if relevant for your location

Receipt of Handbook Received Statement

- [ ] Handbook provided – if digital, show the link to the on-line system
- [ ] Employee understands they must follow policy
- [ ] Who to see with questions
- [ ] Re-state employment at will
- [ ] Employee is responsible to keep up to date with changes and comply
- [ ] Signed and dated by employee

Verify the following:

- [ ] Statement that the handbook is not all inclusive
- [ ] Language allows for flexibility. Words such as generally, often, might for example.
- [ ] If revising an old handbook, state this handbook supersedes any previous handbook provided.
- [ ] Don't make promises that you will not be able to meet in the future
- [ ] Avoid all indication this could be construed as a contract
- [ ] If operating in more than one State, indicate in the handbook which State was used in the writing, but that local law will always take precedence

---

One the pages that follow, you will find a number of sample policies that may be helpful in completing your employee handbook. Be sure to customize each policy for your organization.

Ethics Policy

Writing an ethics policy for your business can be a struggle, but it is important to communicate specifically with employees what is, and is not, acceptable. As a leader, you cannot assume that we all share a common moral compass. Rather, you must set the standard of how we treat others and how you want your employees to make workplace decisions.

Consider the following steps in creating an ethics statement for your organization. Write the statement in your own words. A good ethics statement should reflect the culture of your organization.

Step One

Start with your organizational values. List three items that are non-negotiable in the way you expect employees to behave, make decisions and treat others:

1.

2.

3.

Step Two

Acknowledge that we sometimes have situations that are in conflict with our values. In those cases, what action would you want your employees to take? For example, should they notify someone in the organization, should they make a decision, but let others know. To whom does this apply? Would it be fellow employees, customers, other stake holders?

If you come into conflict with our values, we expect you to take the following steps:

Step Three

Set expectations of ethics through leadership behavior, positive reinforcement and performance management. State in your policy that employees will be evaluated on their ethical performance, and decisions that are not aligned with this policy will not be tolerated. Include ethics in the performance review conversation and ask each manager to report one ethical decision each employee has made as a way to reinforce good decision making.

Step Four

Provide an outlet for employees to discuss concerns without fear of retaliation. While we often state to see your manager, that could be the issue. A complete policy will state 2-3 individuals in various areas of the organization that the employee can discuss issues with who are trained to handle an ethics conversation.

Step Five

After the policy is created, do more than just add it to your handbook. The following ongoing activities are recommended to change behaviors.

1.   Train managers on your policy, expectations and communication

2.   Share the policy and importance with all employees stressing behaviors that are expected

3.   Share outside the organization with stakeholders

4.   Add the formal policy to the employee handbook, post in common areas and electronic media. Consider other appropriate displays such as back of business cards, during company meetings etc.

5.   Celebrate ethical acts out loud, proudly and publicly

6.   Communicate issues of ethical behaviors immediately, privately and with appropriate consequences

Employees today want to work for organizations that set high ethical standards. There is an expectation that leadership will uphold these values on a daily basis. Only your organization knows what they will and won't tolerate. Ethics policies that are communicated and enforced are necessary to keep top talent in today's workforce.

Sample Ethics policy following these guidelines:

Our company holds our ethical standards in the highest regard. We will not tolerate employees who do not respect all whom we interact with, communicate in a way that demonstrates acceptance and makes decisions that are always aligned with legal and moral obligations. There are times where a situation may be difficult to assess. In those instances, please discuss concerns with your supervisor, HR or another member of leadership. We show this through our ongoing leadership and discussion regarding employee performance and growth. If you are faced with behavior from others that you consider to be unethical, please immediately bring that to the attention of your supervisor, HR or another member of leadership. Unethical behavior will not be tolerated and acts found to be in conflict of this policy will be subject to disciplinary action up to and including termination.

Whistleblower Policy

[COMPANY NAME] is committed to high standards of ethical, moral, and legal business conduct. In line with this commitment, and [COMPANY NAME]'s commitment to open communication, we provide an avenue for employees to raise concerns of activity considered to be illegal or dishonest in any dealings during your employment. We do not anticipate you will conduct an investigation or determine fault and you will be protected from reprisals or victimization for reporting any perceived misconduct.

This whistleblowing policy is intended to cover protections for you if you raise concerns regarding activities such as, but not limited to:

- Improper or incorrect financial reporting

- Unlawful activity

- Billing for goods or services not provided

- Behaviors that are not in line with our policies, including business conduct

- Activities, which otherwise are considered to be serious improper conduct

All reports of illegal and dishonest activities should be promptly discussed with your manager, the Director of Finance and Administration, or our Executive Director. In cases where an outside resource is appropriate, contact our Board President or Vice-President. Each of these individuals is responsible for investigating allegations and coordinating corrective action as appropriate.

The whistleblowing procedure is intended to be used for serious and sensitive issues. The earlier a concern is expressed, the easier it is to take action. Although you are not expected to prove the truth of an allegation, you should be able to demonstrate to the person contacted that the report is being made in good faith.

Whistleblower protections are provided in two important areas -- confidentiality and against retaliation. To the extent possible, the confidentiality of the whistleblower will be maintained. However, identity may have to be disclosed to conduct a thorough investigation, to comply with the law and to provide accused individuals their legal rights of defense. [COMPANY NAME] will not retaliate against a whistleblower. This includes, but is not limited to, protection from retaliation in the form of an adverse employment action such as termination, compensation decreases, or poor work assignments and threats of physical harm. Any whistleblower who believes retaliation has occurred must contact the Director of Finance and Administration or Executive Director immediately. The right of a whistleblower for protection against retaliation does not include immunity for any personal wrongdoing that is alleged and investigated.

This policy encourages employees to put their names to allegations because appropriate follow-up questions and investigation may not be possible unless the source of the information is identified. Concerns expressed anonymously will be explored appropriately, but consideration will be given to the seriousness of the issue raised; the credibility of the concern; and the likelihood of confirming the allegation from attributable sources. Allegations in bad faith may result in disciplinary action, including termination.

Employees with any questions regarding this policy should contact the Director of Finance and Administration or the Executive Director.

Antiharassment and Discrimination

Harassment and discrimination are issues that appear in every organization. As hard as we try, we can't control what all of our employees say, how they behave, or how they interpret the actions of others. We respect the rights of employees but have to be sure that our organizations are protected as well.

To ensure clear understanding in our workplaces, legal guidance strongly recommends every employer have an Anti-harassment and Anti-discrimination policy. This should accurately reflect the expectations of your workplace and the actins the company will commit to should there be an issue. An effective and compliant policy will include 5 components:

- A definition of harassment and discrimination. This is often taken directly from the EEOC website.

- Clearly define who is covered under the policy, including those that may not work directly for your organization.

- Explanation of who to report concerns to. This should reference positions not individuals and where possible offer a variety of male and female options.

- Commitment to investigate any claims appropriately for the situation

- Promise of non-retaliation for valid claims

In addition, you should consider ongoing training and communication on the topic to continue to reinforce to your team that this behavior will not be tolerated. A quarterly communication plan will demonstrate that you did not take the topic lightly should it become necessary in legal defense. The communication does not have to be extensive, just consistent. Consider this as a quarterly plan:

- **First Quarter** – Formal training either in person or via webinar

- **Second Quarter** – Email from leadership – let's start the year off right and respect and collaborate with one another.

- **Third Quarter** – Have managers reinforce at department meetings once during quarter

- **Fourth Quarter** – include policy in Annual Open Enrollment materials

On the next page is a sample policy. As with all HR Hacks documents, this is for reference only and should be reviewed with your legal resource.

ANTI-HARASSMENT AND ANTI-DISCRIMINATION POLICY

The Company is committed to a work environment in which all individuals are treated with respect and dignity. Each individual has the right to work in a professional atmosphere that promotes employment opportunities and prohibits unlawful discriminatory practices, including harassment. Therefore, The Company expects that all relationships interacting with our team will be free of bias, prejudice and harassment.

It is the policy of the Company to ensure employment opportunity without discrimination or harassment on the basis of race, color, religion, gender, sexual orientation, gender identity, national origin, age, disability, genetic information, marital status, amnesty or status as a covered veteran; or other segmenting factors protected by law. The Company prohibits any such discrimination or harassment.

Definitions of Harassment

Sexual harassment constitutes discrimination and is illegal under federal, state and local laws. For the purposes of this policy, sexual harassment is defined, as in the Equal Employment Opportunity Commission Guidelines, as unwelcome sexual advances, requests for sexual favors and other verbal or physical conduct of a sexual nature when, for example a) submission to such conduct is made either explicitly or implicitly a term or condition of an individual's employment; b) submission to or rejection of such conduct by an individual is used as the basis for employment decisions affecting such individual; or c) such conduct has the purpose or effect of unreasonably interfering with an individual's work performance or creating an intimidating, hostile or offensive working environment.

Sexual harassment may include a range of subtle and not-so-subtle behaviors and may involve individuals of the same or different gender. Depending on the circumstances, these behaviors may include unwanted sexual advances or requests for sexual favors; sexual jokes and innuendo; verbal abuse of a sexual nature; commentary about an individual's body, sexual prowess or sexual deficiencies; leering, whistling or touching; insulting or obscene comments or gestures; display in the workplace of sexually suggestive objects or pictures; and other physical, verbal or visual conduct of a sexual nature.

Harassment on the basis of any other protected characteristic is also strictly prohibited. Under this policy, harassment is verbal, written or physical conduct that denigrates or shows hostility or aversion toward an individual because of any characteristic protected by law or that of his/her relatives, friends or associates, and that a) has the purpose or effect of creating an intimidating, hostile or offensive work environment; b) has the purpose or effect of unreasonably interfering with an individual's work performance; or c) otherwise adversely affects an individual's employment opportunities.

Individuals and Conduct Covered

These policies apply to all persons who interact with our team, whether related to conduct engaged in by fellow employees or someone not directly connected to the Company (e.g., an outside vendor, consultant or customer). Conduct prohibited by these policies is unacceptable in the workplace and in any work-related setting outside the workplace, such as during business trips, business meetings and business-related social events.

When possible, our company encourages individuals who believe they are being subjected to such conduct to promptly advise the offender that his or her behavior is unwelcome and request that it be discontinued. Often this action alone will resolve the problem. The Company recognizes, however, that an individual may prefer to pursue the matter through complaint procedures.

Complaint Process

Individuals who believe they have been the victims of conduct prohibited by this policy statement or who believe they have witnessed such conduct should discuss their concerns with their immediate supervisor, any member of management, or the President.

The Company encourages the prompt reporting of complaints or concerns so that rapid and constructive action can be taken before relationships become irreparably strained. The Company encourages reporting of all perceived incidents of discrimination or harassment.

Any reported allegations of harassment, discrimination or retaliation will be investigated. The investigation may include individual interviews with the parties involved and, where necessary, with individuals who may have observed the alleged conduct or may have other relevant knowledge. Confidentiality will be maintained throughout the investigatory process to the extent consistent with adequate investigation and appropriate corrective action.

Retaliation against an individual for reporting harassment or discrimination or for participating in an investigation of a claim of harassment or discrimination is a serious violation of this policy and, like harassment or discrimination itself, will be subject to disciplinary action. Acts of retaliation should be reported immediately and will be promptly investigated and addressed.

Misconduct constituting harassment, discrimination or retaliation will be dealt with appropriately. False and malicious complaints of harassment, discrimination or retaliation may be the subject of appropriate disciplinary action.

Telecommuting Policy and Process

Our telecommuting policy will allow workers in positions appropriate to work from home on a (limited, part-time or full-time) basis. This may occur for circumstances such as inclement weather, illness, special projects or business travel. Temporary telecommuting arrangements are approved on an as-needed basis only, with no expectation of ongoing continuance. In case of illness of employee or family member, we may ask for medical confirmation. This does not replace or change your ability to request leave or accommodation under either ADA or FMLA.

The key component to telecommuting is the ability to be productive, interact as needed with the team and serve the clients. For this reason, not every position in the organization will be open to telecommuting. If you feel your position would lend itself to some amount of telecommuting, please speak with your supervisor. We may also choose to utilize telecommuting as an alternative in certain organizational situations and accommodations to particular situations. Telecommuting is not an entitlement, it is not a companywide benefit, and it in no way changes the terms and conditions of employment with our organization.

Telecommuting will begin with approval from your supervisor, human resources and IT. You must be an employee of the organization for more than one year and have an acceptable performance review on file. Any telecommuting arrangement made will be on a trial basis for the first three months and may be discontinued at will and at any time at the request of either the telecommuter or the organization. We will attempt to provide some notice if the arrangement is to end but there may be instances, however, when no notice is possible.

Process

Prior to the telecommuting beginning the following conversations must occur and be approved by HR:

- Established work hours
- Formalize
- Confirm current job description is accurate
- Determine equipment needs and cost
- Review home office location and any liability
- Create quantifiable goals and expectations of performance

Employees entering into this arrangement must agree to;

- Maintain a safe work environment
- Comply with all company rules and processes
- Utilize approved timekeeping process
- Adhere to all IT security measures
- Maintain a secure location for confidential documentation

Action Items for compliance in your organization:

1.	Conduct an assessment of your human resources activities

2.	Allocate a training budget to ensure HR remains up to date on federal, state and local law

3.	Train managers on compliance obligations relevant to your organization

4.	Review employee files

5.	Write or review the current employee handbook

Chapter 3 — Recruiting

Recruiting top talent is an important challenge for all business owners and HR as it's critical to the success of any operation. The full process of recruiting is time consuming and can be fraught with errors. Organizations that do not possess a full-time HR resource find that the time required to identify and engage a new team member can be overwhelming. When there is a single team member responsible for the HR function, recruiting can become a priority leaving other business critical activities to fall to the side. Juggling phone screens, interviews and reference checks can take time away from other critical HR functions. Regardless of whom is responsible, recruiting is a lot of work when done properly.

Consider the recruiting process flows below and on the next pages. First, we show the high-level steps in an effective recruiting process. The next page shows the responsibilities of the various steps to complete the process.

Throughout the remainder of this chapter you will find a variety of tools and templates to complete the various steps and responsibilities for a smooth and effective recruiting process.

Clearly define the position → Market position to candidates → Screen Applicants → Conduct Interviews → Select new team member → Offer position → Onboard new team member

Hiring Process

Recruiting is a process of activities that must be managed at every step. The chart below shows the required steps in an effective recruiting program.

Define need
Determine need for new team member
Review job description for accuracy
Begin draft of job posting

Marketing
Revise job posting
Post ad
Collect resumes and identify qualified candidates
Phone screen candidates

Interviews
Assist in screening
Schedule interviews
Interview candidates
Determine top candidate; inform HR of selection

Selection
Complete reference check(s)
Complete other checks per policy
Determine expected start date and salary
Make offer to candidate
Notify Manager of employee's first day

Onboarding
Return all resumes and applications to HR
Notify team of new employee
Call to welcome new team member after acceptance
Prepare for first day and week

Compliance issues faced when recruiting

Throughout the search process, compliance rears its ugly head again! There are several laws that impact the recruiting cycle that you must be aware of. Below are some parts of the recruiting puzzle that can run afoul of the law.

__*Marketing the position*__ – be aware of the wording used in ads. You cannot use words that would discriminate or deter a candidate from applying based on any criteria in Title VII, or other segments of the population that may be protected by law. Some examples of protected categories include age, gender, religion, etc.

__*Interview Questions*__ – all questions must be job-related and unbiased. You should ask similar questions of all candidates. The questions should not elicit information that would lead to discriminatory information being shared. Some examples of topics that you **should not** inquire about include:

Medical condition	Disability
Genetic Information	Marital status or if they have children
National Origin	Group Membership
Age	(other than job related)
Citizenship	Gender
Arrest Record	Sexual Orientation

__*Americans with Disabilities Act*__ – applies to candidates as well as employees. Interview space must be accessible to those with disabilities; and candidates can only be asked if they can complete the essential functions of the job with or without accommodation.

__*Citizenship*__ – A candidate cannot be asked about their citizenship, only their ability to legally work in the United States. An I-9 form cannot be completed until after an employee has been offered a position. Once hired, the I-9 must be completed within 72 hours of starting work.

__*Background and credit checks*__ – In general, there must be a job-related basis for conducting background or credit checks. There are several state laws that govern this area; be sure to check before completing any investigation.

__*Pre-employment testing*__ – concerns exist with tests' reliability and accuracy in predicting success of a candidate. For this reason, you should always use tests that are professionally marketed and guaranteed to be compliant with the Equal Employment Opportunity Commission.

__*Medical exam and drug testing*__ – candidates cannot be subject to any medical testing, including a drug test, until the job is offered.

__*Ban the box*__ –This concept states that you may not ask questions about criminal history on the employment application. Currently it is regulated at the state and local level. Be sure to determine if your State allows this question.

Size of the candidate pool

The candidate funnel works just like a sales funnel. If you want to hire one great employee, you need to consider many candidates. The illustration below will change for each organization and position, but the idea is the same.

Initial Applicants
Candidates that have applied to your original ad
Receive 100

Qualifed Applicants
After a quick initial screen, those that have the qualifications that seem appropriate to you
Select 30

Phone Screens
After reviewing those qualified, which seem to be a good fit
Set up 20; Conduct 12

Interviews
Meets initial qualifications on phone screen and seem interested in position
Invite 6-8

Possible Hires
Viable candidates; all of whom can do the job
Identify 3

New Employee

Getting Started

Not so fast! A departing team member gives management the perfect opportunity to step back and evaluate what the organization really needs moving forward. When a team member leaves, evaluate the workload of other employees:

- the impact technology may have had on the position

- others that are cross trained

- interest of internal candidates

- fit of this position with the rest of the department

- ability for this to be a part time or flexible work schedule

- are you willing to consider remote employees

- possibility of outsourcing

Take the time to assess the position and the needs of the organization to determine what the next step should be.

Analyze the criteria used in the past and consider if this is still applicable. Give thought to aspects such as new skills required, use of technology, and interaction with customers. Compensation requirements in the market may have changed as well. If the departing employee was with your organization for several years, their salary may be reflective of annual increases or acquired cross-training. Current market rates for the same skills may be less than you had been paying.

Start with a thorough analysis of the job as it is today. The job assessment template on the next page will help you think through all the elements of the position you need to fill. This exercise is especially helpful if you are creating a new position. Use this information to complete the formal job description which is on the page following the position profile.

Once this is completed, you will be ready to move forward with the search for your new team member.

Position Recruitment Profile

Hiring Manager:		Phone:	
Work location for position:		E-mail:	
Others to be involved in the process:			

Position/Job Title:		Department:	
Reason position is being filled:		Salary Range:	
Work Hours:		Is Overtime required:	
Is travel out of area required?		What is the dress code?	

What specific skills will be required?

Is there a preferred level of education desired?

What previous experience would you expect to see on a candidate's resume?

Are there key words to look for on the candidate's resume?

Give a short summary of the position:

List 3-5 primary duties of this position:

Primary Function	Approx. hours per week	Necessary skills

Who will this person interact with most often?

What are some qualities you would expect to find in an "ideal" candidate?

What would describe the "wrong" candidate?

List 2-3 critical goals for the first 90 days and year?
90 days:
One Year:

Describe someone who has been effective in this position in the past and what made them effective.

What would you say is the biggest challenge the new employee will face?

Are there other areas your new hire will be expected to back up and or support?

What does the employee need to know, and what training is required?

Computer Skills:

Special Skills Required:

Job Description

Use this template to insert the relevant issues for this position. Notes on considerations for each section are shown in italics.

JOB DESCRIPTION

Job Title:		Department:	
Exempt/Non-exempt:	*insert the appropriate designation under the Fair Labor Standards Act – see chapter 6*	Full, Part Time or Seasonal:	
Location:		Travel Required:	
Education Anticipated:	*Be sure that education is reflective of the skills needed to complete the job. Always consider adding "or equivalent experience" to the requirement*		
Special Skills:	*Specific software, language, industry etc. needed for the position.*		

OVERVIEW:

Provide a 3-4 sentence description of the position including the purpose as it impacts the overall organization.

ESSENTIAL FUNCTIONS OF POSITION:

- *List the top 8-10 functions of the position. This is not intended to be a laundry list of every task that needs to be accomplished, rather an overview of the key components that will define success in the role.*

- *Always have the last function state "and all other duties requested by management"*

DESIRED COMPETENCIES:

In today's world, the functions of the job are often a small part of what we look for in employees. Competencies are those softer skills that can be difficult to define, but are critical to success in a position. Including competencies in your job descriptions is an effective way to start the conversation around expectations as well as holding employees accountable for performance in these areas.

Competencies that are often used in organizations include:

- *Communication*

- *Customer Service*

- *Leadership*

- *Innovation*

- *Problem Solving skills*

QUALIFICATIONS AND EDUCATION REQUIREMENTS:

- *Be specific as to what is needed to complete the role. This is a section that will be reviewed closely should there ever be a claim of discrimination, so it must accurately reflect what is necessary to be successful. This can be a bulleted list or 2-3 sentences.*

- *This section may be more specific than the above "Special skills" for what you are looking for. For instance, knowledge of Microsoft Office may be a qualification, but not really rise to the level of a special skill.*

PHYSICAL REQUIREMENTS:

In this section, it is essential that your requirements are necessary for the position. Physical requirements are the basis used for workers compensation and discrimination claims in many cases. Confirm what is required for the position is accurate. When we consider physical requirements think about the actual need to:

- *Hear – speak to others in the office and use a telephone*
- *Speak – does this role require ongoing communication with others that can't be handled in another other way?*
- *Stand/sit – how long during the day does a person need to be able to do these things*
- *Use hands/fingers – most often this will relate to the need to use a computer keyboard and paper files you may have etc. Often very applicable in manufacturing environments*
- *Lifting requirements – this is generally stated as the number of pounds an employee is able to lift. It is imperative that this is a real ongoing need for the position. If 2-3 times a month a box of copy paper needs to be moved, it is unlikely a real requirement for the position as someone else can help do that for the employee on occasion.*

Any requirement you state should obviously a part of the position, or be vetted by occupational health or medical professionals to ensure compliance with all laws.

Approved By:		Date:	
Employee Signature:		Date:	

Think outside the box when recruiting. Recruiting for a new hire is no different than marketing your product to customers. You should consider where the candidates are and what will get them excited about joining your team. When we train managers to fill the candidate pipeline, we discuss 5 opportunities to uncover top talent as shown below.

- Social Media

- Internal candidates

- Employee referral programs

- Educational institutions

- Networking

The placement of your marketing efforts should be specific to the industry, position, and other criteria that define the ideal candidate. For instance, you would not advertise for a new CFO the same way you would look for a manufacturing employee.

Social Media

The most common formal recruiting today is done through social media and the Internet. The most commonly used posting sites are Indeed and LinkedIn. Craigslist® can also be a good source of candidates for hourly and entry-level positions. The key to managing the online community is having an application process that will not overwhelm the HR administrator or hiring manager. When possible, set up a dedicated email address for job inquiries. If recruiting is a regular part of your operation, consider an applicant tracking system. Affordable, basic systems are available from many payroll service vendors and will integrate with their systems for reporting. You can also purchase stand-alone software or utilize the functionality from the major job boards.

Internal candidates

You are not required to consider current employees for an opening or post positions you may have available. However, moving a current employee to a new role can be a very effective way to provide growth and retain top talent. Filling a critical position with someone whose character and skills you are familiar with is often advantageous to the continuity of your business.

If a current employee is interested but not qualified, have an open and honest conversation about the skills that are lacking. Work with the employee to provide training opportunities so they are eligible in the future.

Moving a top performer can be a strain on the current role they occupy, but you should not hold an employee back from a promotion opportunity just because it will be difficult to replace them. Employees that see no growth or opportunities for promotion will soon leave your organization. Better to retain the talent and have them help train their replacement.

In evaluating internal candidates answer the following:

- Is the interested employee a top performer?
- What training will the person need?
- How will you fill the position they are vacating?

Caution: Do not move a poor performer into another role unless you are certain the new position is a better fit. If you are transitioning a team member that has not been successful, have an open and honest conversation about what success will look like in the new position. Provide clear consequences if they are not able to meet those expectations.

Employee referral programs

Employee referral programs can be the strongest tool in your organization to find top talent. We know that employees only refer those people that they would be excited to work with. Their reputation is on the line, and they are going to have to work side by side with the new employee. If the candidate is not exceptional, they are not likely to want to bring them to work with them. To make a program work, it must be meaningful to employees. At the same time, you need to be sure it drives results.

A template to help you create your own employee referral program follows in this section.

Educational Institutions

Connect with a local community college or university that provides training in your industry. Find a program that aligns with your business and meet the head of the department. Ask for introductions to the instructors and offer to lecture or provide tours of your operation. They know their students need to connect with the real world. Keep an ongoing dialogue and support the program throughout the year. Once they get to know you and your team, they can become a great source of part-time and permanent employees.

Networking

When looking for a professional or managerial candidate, word of mouth and networking is an excellent place to start. Your perfect hire might not be on LinkedIn or Twitter, but a friend or family member might let them know the position is available. Announce the position to your trusted advisors and networking community as a first step.

Complete the chart on the next page to give additional thought to which recruiting source will work best for your organization.

Recruitment Marketing Opportunities

Consider the various columns for each position you need to fill.

Position:_____

Placement	Effectiveness	My Access	Cost	Likelihood of finding candidates
Internal Candidates	Shows ability to move up in your organization; great for retention			
Active Candidates Those looking for new position	Easy to reach, can be quick to find			
Passive Candidates Those that may be interested, but not actively looking	More effort required to find, but possibly top-notch candidates			
Networking Organizations Vendors	Can take longer, but may result in highly recommended candidate			
Social Media LinkedIn post Facebook Twitter Instagram	Could be very quick, highly recommended talent – but also promoting to those you may not want!			
Internet sites Indeed.com craigslist® LinkedIn paid ad Monster Career Builder Industry sites	Cost can be a factor. Set a budget and understand speed can be a factor. There are new sites on the scene every day – one good tip is to google the job you are advertising and see what other sites come up!			
Employee Referral program	Excellent way to find top talent – example on the next page			
Alumni Network	Ask former employees for recommendations – or to return!			
Educational Institutions	Connect with instructors to get referrals of their best students			

Employee Referral Program

Create a program that is meaningful to employees and be sure that you publish it. A successful program will help you find the best new members of your team with minimal risk.

Suggestions for a successful employee referral program:

The program must be publicized often! You can't just put it in the employee handbook and forget about it.

- Have a policy/program outline in your employee handbook.
- When there is a job opening, send a notice to employees reminding them to have their networks apply.
- Once someone makes a recommendation and their contact is hired, provide the award publicly and thank them for participating.
- When you announce the new hire – remind your team that they were referred by your current team member.

Understand your current cost of recruiting

- Where do you typically advertise positions? What is the cost?
- How much time does it take to sift through resumes?
- Referral will typically shorten the phone screen, but all other time spent is the same.

Create a program that drives the results you want

- Is there a particular position that is more difficult to hire?
- Would you like to increase longevity of employees?
- The program should be written and clearly explain that candidates must be selected as the best fit for the position and those referred are not guaranteed a position.

Steps for creating the actual program

- The employment application should ask if a candidate has been referred by an employee.
- The current employee should notify the hiring manager of a referral and introduce the applicant to the organization.
- An employee making a recommendation should not be involved in the hiring process.
- Provide an award that will incentivize your employees. Consider the cost of hiring and the increased confidence in the hire.
- Stretch the award over time to ensure long term success.
- Management should notify the employee whether the recommended candidate was hired AFTER the candidate is selected or rejected.
- Determine if there are fields in your payroll system to trigger the payments due to the employee(s) at the proper time.

Caution points

- Watch diversity. Referral programs tend to replicate your current workforce.
- Employees could be angry if their recommended candidate doesn't get the job.
- As an organization, decide which managers may or may not participate in the program.
- Significant incentives are considered taxable compensation.

Writing a Great Ad

The goal of a job ad is to create a pool of qualified candidates that are all qualified and meet the needs of the position. You can evaluate the pool quickly to select the top candidates to interview. Using the steps below, you will be able to create a customized ad quickly and effectively for any open position.

Advertising for an employee is similar to the marketing process. You must create an ad that will invite the best candidates to apply. At the same time, you want to ensure that you discourage those that are not qualified from applying. The ad needs to reflect your organization and give the job seekers the information they need to make the decision to apply.

When writing your ad, evaluate these points before you begin:

- **Determine how the ad will reflect your culture (add other words that describe)**
    - Casual or formal
    - Fun or professional
    - Creative or process oriented
    - _____
    - _____
    - _____

- **List three key words that will attract the candidates**
    - _____
    - _____
    - _____

- **Define the qualifications that are essential**
    - _____
    - _____
    - _____

- **Consider those qualifications that would be nice to have in a candidate**
    - _____
    - _____
    - _____

- **Key points about the company/position that would be important for candidates**
    - Industry _____
    - Location _____
    - Hours _____
    - Size of organization _____
    - Who they report to _____
    - Growth or flexibility _____
    - Salary _____
    - Consider a broad range to all for many levels to apply, but eliminate those that need a salary outside your range

Writing the ad...

1. **Write a headline with a hook. Make it clear and relevant to the job seeker.**

    For example: looking to take your (insert position) career to the next level?

    Your headline: _____

2. **State the benefits of reading further**

    For example: We offer the right candidate an opportunity to be a part of a decision-making team and learn new skills. Our casual environment provides creativity and flexibility to take your career to the next level.

    Write the next few lines of your ad with key terms that are relevant to the job seeker:

    _____

3. **Provide an overview of the position – in 2-3 sentences explain the highlights. Include the key words you highlighted on the previous page.**

    How would you describe the key elements of this position:

    _____

    _____

    _____

4. **Tell a little about the company – this is not a place to brag. Use the elements outlined in the worksheet – 2-3 sentences are appropriate for this section.**

    Our company (Company Name)...

    _____

    _____

    _____

5. **List the requirements of the position**

    We expect qualified candidates to have:

    _____

    Outstanding candidates will also have these preferred qualifications:

    _____

6. **Contact information**: How will you be receiving resumes?

    _____

Review the final ad for:

- Culture fit
- Intriguing to job seeker
- Accurate reflection of position
- Clearly defined qualifications
- Easy to read
- Contact information

Evaluating Applicants for a Successful Fit

On initial review, the resume or application should be error-free and well organized. These are the two common traits we expect of all applicants, regardless of the position for which they are being considered. If candidates are willing to submit a resume or application with spelling mistakes, imagine the quality of their work when they secure a position.

Don't put too much weight on the professionalism of the résumé. Some candidates have access to resources of professional writers that are not available to others. It should be clean, error free and organized.

Your focus should be on the skills, history and qualifications of the applicant.

Checklist to be used when evaluating the initial candidate pool

Area of Interest	Notes to consider	Importance for this position
Basic skills required	Look for the minimum skills that cannot be trained	
Desired Education	Differentiate between required and preferred	
Experience	Is it transferrable, not identical, to your position	
Progression in job(s)	Do the job titles/tasks show increased responsibility	
Consistent work history	Look for job gaps, can they be explained?	
Error free	Are there mistakes that should have been obvious	
Well Organized	Is it easy to follow the flow	

Phone Screens do have a Purpose!

Time is precious – for you and the candidate. Often you have non-negotiable criteria for a position that can be quickly discussed on the phone to be sure an in-person interview is productive for all. Topics to explore often include salary, location, hours, questions on resume and candidates desire for a new position. Using the questions below, cover these issues before setting up an in-person interview.

1.	What are your salary expectations?
a.	If they refuse to answer, ask for a range.

2.	Is our location convenient for you?
a.	Mention whether you are convenient to public transportation, have free or paid parking etc.

3.	What is causing you to look for a new job at this time?
a.	Be sure they are looking for what you are offering

4.	Review skills that are "must have" for your next hire

5.	Discuss gaps in employment

6.	Describe the parts of your current role that you enjoyed most/least

7.	Explore what is important to the candidate in their next position

After the conversation, determine if you feel the match is close enough to continue the conversation. If so, move them to the list to be scheduled for an interview.

Don't schedule the candidate during the phone screen. When you are screening several candidates, someone can seem to be perfect at the beginning of the search but will move to a "maybe" group later. If the candidate is not a good fit, simply thank them for their time and say that you will get back to them.

Always let candidates know if they are not moving forward in the process within a week of the phone screen. Most electronic applicant systems allow you to send an electronic message that can simply say:

"Thank you for your time. At this time, we are not moving forward with your application. Best of luck in your job search."

This is a quick, easy and professional way of ending your relationship with the candidate.

Employment Applications

Most candidates will arrive for an interview with resume in hand. There are also many positions for which a resume is not the typical way of applying. Regardless of the candidate's expectations, it is always prudent to have each candidate complete an employment application that you have customized for your organization.

The application will serve many purposes including:

- All candidates are on a level playing field in terms of information provided/gathered

- You will be sure all questions you have are answered

- There is a paragraph of information that candidates agree to comply with

- Managers can quickly scan the form with which they are familiar

- Documentation of the employee's responses and date of application

On the following pages, we provide tools for you to evaluate your current form, as well as a sample form to be used.

Employment Applications

Use this checklist to review common components of a current employment application you may be using today.

Items	Notes	Yes	No
Collecting social security number	There is no reason to have for every applicant. Given the issues with identify theft, it is no longer recommended to be on the application. You will collect for those hired as needed.		
Email address	It is perfectly acceptable to communicate via email, and candidates prefer it.		
Question regarding previous criminal activity	Be very careful with the "Ban the box" rules. If you are unsure about the regulations in your state, check with the Department of Labor, or omit all questions at the application stage for ensured compliance.		
Previous Salary	Laws are being passed by States making it illegal to ask candidates about past salary. If that is true in your State, eliminate the question from your application. You can ask desired salary for a position on the application.		
Education	Do not request date of completion. This has been used to initiate age discrimination cases.		
Gender	States are starting to require options beyond the typical male/female. Consider if gender is even a necessary question on your application.		
Citizenship	You must carefully word "are you eligible to work in the United States". You cannot specifically ask if a person is a citizen in most cases.		
Statement regarding policies, honesty at interview etc.	This block should contain language regarding honesty at the interview, employment at will, and policies that are critical to your business.		
Signature and date	Be sure the candidate signs and dates the application.		

On the following pages, you will find a template for an employment application that can be customized for your organization.

Application for Employment

Candidate's Name:		Date:	
Address:			
Telephone Number:		Email address:	

Are you authorized to work in the U.S.? .... ☐ Yes ☐ No

Have you ever worked or attended school under another name? If so, under what name?

General Information

Position Desired:		Wage rate desired:	

Do you prefer: ☐ Full-time ☐ Part-time *If part-time, hours per week desired*:

Are you able to work: ☐ 9-5 Monday – Friday ☐ Holidays ☐ Night ☐ Overtime ☐ Week-ends

How did you learn about this opening?
Indicate if an employee referred you to this position

Education

High School:	Graduated? ☐ Yes ☐ No	Course of Study:
Technical School:	Graduated? ☐ Yes ☐ No	Course of Study:
College/University:	Graduated? ☐ Yes ☐ No	Course of Study:
Post-Graduate Education:	Graduated? ☐ Yes ☐ No	Course of Study:

Other education, certification, training or special skills:

Skills

Are you experienced in using personal computers?   ☐ Yes ☐ No   ☐ PC ☐ Mac

What other skills should we be aware of:

Work Experience

> *Please list all previous employment, beginning with the most recent. If you need more room, you may attach another sheet of paper or your resume.*

Employer:		City, State:
Dates of employment:	Position Held:	Reason for Leaving:
Supervisor's Name & Title:		May we contact? ☐ Yes ☐ No
Description of Duties:		

Employer:		City, State:
Dates of employment:	Position Held:	Reason for Leaving:
Supervisor's Name & Title:		May we contact? ☐ Yes ☐ No
Description of Duties:		

Employer:		City, State:
Dates of employment:	Position Held:	Reason for Leaving:
Supervisor's Name & Title:		May we contact? ☐ Yes ☐ No
Description of Duties:		

Authorization and Acknowledgements

I affirm that the information I have provided in this application is true to the best of my knowledge, information, and belief, and I have not knowingly withheld any information requested. I understand that withholding or misstating any information requested in this application is a ground for rejection of my application, and if hired is grounds for discharge. This is true of information provided during the interview process as well. This application is valid for 30 days, after that time I must reapply for consideration.

I authorize **Company Name** to verify my references, record of employment, education record, and any other information I have provided. Unless otherwise noted, I authorize the references I have listed to disclose any information related to my work record and my professional experiences with them, without giving me prior notice of such disclosure. In addition, I release the company, my former employers and all other persons and entities, from any and all claims, demands or liabilities arising out of or in any way related to such inquiry or disclosure.

If I am hired, I understand that either **Company Name** or I can terminate my employment at any time and for any reason, with or without cause and without prior notice. I understand that no representative of **Company Name** has the authority to make any assurance to the contrary.

Once employed I will be provided with the company policies and understand it is my obligation to obey and stay up to date on policies. These policies may include drug testing and the ability to view my electronic communications as related to the company. Only the President or CEO can make changes to policy or promises to me regarding my employment.

_____   _____

Candidate's Signature   Date

Conducting the Interview

The interview begins the minute the candidate arrives at your location. Don't minimize the importance of the time they arrive, how they act in the parking lot and especially how they treat your receptionist or other employees. These are all situations in which they think they are not being evaluated and will show you their real personality.

You must determine in advance who will participate in the interview. There are advantages and disadvantages to a variety of interview methods. The chart on the next page details a few common techniques. Which will work best for your organization is up to you. There is no right or wrong, and will likely fluctuate based on the position.

Many managers prefer the team be involved in the hiring process. Use caution when involving team members in what is referred to as "committee style" interviews. Involving team members can create an unwritten contract that everyone will have a vote. While it is not uncommon, it can lead to a group settling for a candidate that all can live with, rather than selecting the very best candidate to do the job. Managers should always have the last word on the candidate selection.

Panel interviews are a good alternative. This is an interview style where current employees are invited to attend and ask questions based on their areas of expertise. They provide feedback to the managers and answer specific questions for the candidate. In a panel interview, participants are asked for input but are not involved in the final decision making.

An effective combination of interview selection methods is to have a manager interview all the candidates one-on-one. For a final interview, bring back the top candidate and have them meet the team. Let the team know the manager has made the selection, and unless there is a glaring red flag during the final meeting, the manager will move forward. Candidates have often amazed their future co-workers with what that say! In this scenario, the manager has the final decision, but co-workers do have a chance to weigh in and voice their opinion, especially if there is a concern.

Types of interviews

Interview Method	Description	Advantages	Disadvantages
One-on-One	Manager meets the candidate alone	• Personal connection • Easy to schedule • Discuss changes • Candidate most comfortable	• Candidate only hears one perspective • No buy-in from team members • Miss critical information
Committee Interview	Team participates each with an equal vote	• Multiple opinions • Team agrees on candidate • Candidate can meet future co-workers	• Team may not all have same goals in mind • Settle on candidate that is acceptable to all
Panel Interview	Team participates but manager makes final decision	• Experts in various areas can question candidate • Candidate meets future co-workers • Manager is primary decision maker	• Each person asking questions on expertise, confusing for candidates • Time commitment from many people

Format of an Interview

Virtual interviews are becoming more and more popular. Consider if you have more flexibility conducting your interviews via a video platform as an option. Whether in person or virtual, your interview should follow a routine and last about 40-60 minutes. However, if you quickly realize this is not a fit, feel free to excuse yourself and the candidate. Be sure that you are ending the interview for a concrete reason, such as the candidate being unqualified. I have had many interviews begin poorly only to find the candidate perfect at the end.

Welcome (3-5 min)

Start by making the candidate comfortable. Ask if they found the location easily, would they like water, introduce yourself etc.

Do not tell them a great deal about the organziation or the position. You will want to see what they have found out on their own later

Let them know a bit about the process, and there will be time at the end for them to ask questions

Applicant History (8-15 min)

Review resume
Ask about gaps in employment
Which position did they enjoy and why
Why are they looking for new position now
Discuss any skill gaps

Interview Questions (10 – 15 min)

Behaviorally based interview questions. See next page for details

Discuss position (3-5 min)

Tell them a bit about the position
Let them know your expectations for a successful team member
Be honest about any "less desirable" parts of the job

Ask if they have questions for you (5-7 min)

They should have done some homework and have a few prepared questions
Allow them to ask a few, but also control the time if they have a very long list
Let them know if you are not the right person to answer

Let them know next steps (2-3 min)

Be specific and honest about when you'll be back in touch with them
Do not tell them at this time if they are moving forward in the process
Let them know what the next step is in the process and when you'll be in contact

Behavior Based Interview Questions

As shown on the page before, you will typically have 40 – 60 minutes to determine whether a candidate will be someone you want on your team. In this short amount of time, it is difficult to determine everything you want to know with certainty. The idea of taking the time to craft great interview questions is to ensure that you are using the time to gather the information you need to make a long-term decision.

Research has proven the best way to gain an understanding of how a candidate may perform in your environment is to ask about how they have performed in similar situations in the past. This is referred to as the behavioral based interview technique. Avoid asking common interview questions that the candidate may have practiced in advance or those that only produce a yes or no answer. The idea of the interview is to get the candidate talking about the way they work and what is important to them in a position. Only then can you evaluate if they are a good fit for the position and your culture.

Think about some of the common questions below, and the recommended behavioral interview question to replace them.

Typical question	Behavioral replacement
What are your strengths?	Tell me about an accomplishment in the past year you are especially proud of and what steps you took to make it happen.
What are your weaknesses?	What is one item on your past performance review that your manager felt needed work and what did you do to improve?
How do you get along in a team?	Describe the last team project you were on. What was your role and how did it go?
What motivates you?	Tell me about the last time you worked really hard to achieve something. What was the reward and why was it important to you?

Good questions are those that ask for the patterns of behavior taken in the past. There is no right or wrong answer to a behavioral question. The idea is to understand how the candidate acted at a point in time and if that's a fit with your culture. There are three components to a behavioral interview question:

- Situation or task candidate was faced with
- Action Taken
- Results of the action

Use the charts on the next page to practice creating a few behavioral based questions that you can ask of all candidates. Think of those topics that will be important to your organization regardless of position such as teamwork, communication, attendance etc.

A few behavioral questions that can be used generically include:

- Tell me about a stressful situation you faced and how you handled it.
- We all have deadlines we miss. Tell me about one you knew you were not going to make and how you got the project done.
- Give me an example of a time you were not happy about the decision the group or company made and how you voiced your opinion.
- Has there been a time that you worked really hard for a special prize or reward?

Example for the need to find a candidate who will think independently:

Position: Reception	Your Question
Situation or task	Tell me about a time you were faced with a problem
Action	and your manager was out of the office.
Results	How did you proceed and what solution did you come up with?

Now create questions for your position:

Position:	Your Question
Situation or task	
Action	
Results	

Position:	Your Question
Situation or task	
Action	
Results	

Sample Interview Questions

Below is a sample of interview questions that follow the principals on the previous pages that can be used generically for many positions.

- Tell me about something you had to work hard to accomplish last year and how you did it?

- What was an issue for improvement on your recent performance review and how did you improve?

- Describe the most difficult manager you ever worked for. How did you handle the relationship?

- We are all late sometimes. Tell me about a time you knew you weren't going to arrive at work on time (or at all) and what you did.

- Tell me about a really stressful work situation you faced in the past year and how you handled it.

- Describe a situation when you had two customers who needed something that they each felt was urgent. How did you handle each person?

- Tell me about something really difficult you were asked to do at one of your last few jobs and how you went about accomplishing it.

- What was something in the last year you needed to learn how to do – and how did you go about learning it?

- Tell me about starting your last position. What was the most helpful part of your first week? What do you wish they would have done differently?

- What was the best team you were a part of? Why?

- Tell me about a time someone trained you to do something new – what worked best for you?

- Describe the work environment at your last position. What did you like most and least?

- Who was the best manager you ever worked for? What about this manager was so effective for you?

- When you have worked in groups or teams, describe the role you have taken on.

- Can you provide an example of how you have helped promote a company in the past?

- Tell me about a time you represented your organization in the community or with a non-profit activity.

Common Interview Mistakes

When you don't conduct interviews often it's easy to treat the meeting similar to other business meetings you have when you meet a new vendor or make sales calls. For an interview, you want the candidate to do most of the talking so you can listen and learn. Here are other common mistakes made when interviewing.

INTERVIEWER MISTAKE	WHAT SHOULD YOU DO?
Not being prepared for the interview	Read the candidate's resume before the interview. Prepare a few important questions to elicit the information you are seeking. Remember, this is your chance to find the talent you are seeking, so give it the attention it deserves.
Talking too much (80/20 Rule)	Listen…. Listen…Listen! Let the candidate do most of the talking. You are there to learn about the candidate.
"Giving Away" too much information early in the interview	Providing a great deal of information early in the interview will allow the candidate to formulate answers that work for the organization, not necessarily an accurate reflection of themselves.
Keeping the candidate waiting	Be on time. Give the candidate the respect that you expect in return. No one likes having to wait.
Answering your telephone or checking email	Give the interviewee 100% of your attention. Turn off your computer and silence your cell phone.
Excessive note taking	Listen more and write less. Note key points and then elaborate after the interview.
Rapid fire questions	Have patience. Give the candidate a chance to think and answer questions.
Setting unrealistic expectations	Be honest with yourself and the candidate. No one will fit the mold perfectly. Understand the "deal breaker" skills and be willing to compromise.
Outside interruptions	Sit in an area that is free from distractions. This may mean moving out of your office where everyone knows where to find you. Consider using a conference room where you are less likely to be interrupted.
Asking "Yes" or "No" questions	Ask open-ended questions that encourage candidates to express themselves using specific examples.

Legal Interview Questions

Many interview questions can be construed as illegal. It is essential that the questions you ask do not impact any discrimination law. These are the laws that typically apply to race, age, gender, national origin, marital status, and disability.

- Ask only job-related questions.

- To the extent possible, ask all candidates the same questions.

- Avoid topics that would lead to information in areas that may elicit discriminatory information.

- Understand state and local law as well.

TOPIC	DISCRIMINATORY	LEGAL TO ASK
FAMILY STATUS	✖ Are you married? ✖ What does your spouse do for a living? ✖ Do you prefer Miss, Ms., or Mrs.? ✖ Are you pregnant? ✖ What are your childcare arrangements?	✔ The job requires 50% travel. Is there anything that would prevent you from meeting this requirement? ✔ Your regular workday will be 12:00 PM – 8:00 PM. Will that cause any conflicts for you?
RACE	✖ What is your race?	✔ None
RELIGION	✖ What is your religion?	✔ None, but you can ask if a candidate can work specific hours if necessary.
RESIDENCE	✖ Do you rent or own your home? ✖ Who resides with you?	✔ What is your address?
AGE	✖ How old are you? ✖ What is your birthday?	✔ If hired, can you offer proof that you are at least working age?
PHYSICAL CONDITIONS	✖ Are you disabled? ✖ What is the nature or severity of your disability? ✖ Do you have health issues? ✖ What drugs are you taking?	✔ Must follow the job description – for example: This job requires lifting boxes weighing up to 60 lbs. Can you perform this function with or without reasonable accommodations?
SEX	✖ Are you male or female?	✔ None
CITIZENSHIP	✖ Are you a U.S. citizen? ✖ Where were you born?	✔ Can you show proof of your eligibility to work in the US?
ORGANIZATIONS	✖ What organizations do you belong to?	✔ What job-relevant organizations are you a member of?
CRIMINAL HISTORY	✖ Have you ever been arrested?	✔ Have you ever been convicted of a felony?
EMERGENCY NOTIFICATION	✖ Whom should we notify in case of an emergency? ✖ What is their relationship to you?	✔ None, until they are hired.
EDUCATION	✖ When did you attend/ graduate?	✔ What schools did you attend? ✔ Did you graduate?
LANGUAGE	✖ What is your native language?	✔ Do you write or speak any languages other than English?

Completing the interview process

The final candidate selected should undergo an appropriate background check process. Your organization must determine what that means, and the process will often differ for each position.

For the reference check, consider utilizing the form provided on the next page. Print on your company letterhead and complete the data you have available from the resume or application. The form can be scanned and sent via email to a reference provided, or you can call and take the information over the phone. Retain a copy of the completed form for each former employer.

The chart below provides recommended guidelines on reference and background checks.

Verification	Notes	How	Cost
Formal background check by outside organization	This is a full scope typically used to check all aspects including criminal history, past employers, education etc.	Utilize a professional background check company. Easily found on internet, or reach out to HR Topics for suggestions.	Full check of all areas listed will be $125 – $250 depending on scope
Former Employers	ALWAYS check candidates past 5-7 years of employment. Ideally speak to their supervisor, but if not, confirm dates of employment, position and if they are eligible for rehire.	A quick call to the employer is all you need to confirm past employment. On the next page, we provide a template for a telephone or written verification.	Minimal apart from the time involved. Some employers are now using outside services for response, so there could be a cost up to $20 per employer.
Education	If a degree is required, call the College or University to confirm graduation. In most cases, confirm only the highest level of education to ensure a truthful resume.	Most colleges and universities will accept a call to the Registrar's office. Be sure that you have a social security number available. Ask all applicants for their name at time of graduation.	Some educational institutions are now using outside services for response, so there could be a cost; generally not more than $30.
Credit check	Use carefully and primarily only with those positions where access to cash or credit card information is an issue. Be especially careful to check your state law for this area. Understand your obligations under the Fair Credit Reporting Act.	ONLY use an authorized background check provider. NEVER ask a candidate for their credit score or any other credit information. This is often completed in conjunction with a full background check.	Minimal, generally under $20 to check credit only, generally part of full background check.

Employment Verification Form

To: _____

Date: _____

I, ___(insert candidate name)__, am applying for a position and would appreciate your completing this form to allow them to move forward with my application.

Written Name:_____   Signature:_____

You have been indicated as a former employer, and we'd like to confirm the facts below prior to making a job offer.

We are holding the job offer awaiting your information, so quick completion is appreciated!

Thank you,

Your Name

Candidate was employed by your organization from _____ until_____.

Title: _____

Salary at time of departure: _____

Would performance be considered:

☐ Excellent   ☐ Good   ☐ Fair   ☐ Below expectations

Is this employee eligible for rehire?   ☐ Yes   ☐ No

If no, please explain _____

_____

Additional Comments: _____

_____

_____

Are any facts above incorrect?

_____

_____

Verified by: _____

Title: _____

Please return completed form to:_____ at _____

Closing out the recruiting process

It is best practice that you notify all candidates when they are no longer being considered for the position. General practice recommends waiting 24 – 48 hours after a phone or in-person interview. You don't want to send it as they are walking out the door! An email note is fine; candidates are pleased with any communication, so they know where they stand.

Most advertising and applicant tracking systems can send the email for you through an automated process. Templates are set up with the information you want to communicate. They can be personalized so the candidate feels they are receiving a personalized communication from the organization. When you have this type of system, it is easy and polite to reply to each applicant with a short note.

The important point about your letter is to be very general about the status of their application. Candidates have used specific notes to challenge the basis of their candidacy and you don't want to open that door. Use the communication to let them know they are no longer being considered.

Do not promise to keep their application on file or consider them in the future. This creates a legal obligation to do so. If you haven't met them in person, there is no need to sign your name, simply because you don't want them calling you!

Caution: Always hold off notifying your second choice until the candidate you want has accepted the position. Often you will need to make the offer to the second choice and you wouldn't want them to know they were #2.

On the next page, you will find three templates that can be used in various situations during the interview process to notify candidates that they are no longer being considered. Do not provide information regarding why they were not selected or make a commitment to review their application in the future.

Examples of contact with candidates:

For a resume that you are not moving forward:

Thank you for applying for the _____ position at _____ company. At this time, we are unable to move forward with your application. Best of luck in your job search.

Human Resources at Company name

After a phone interview:

I appreciate the time you spent on the phone with me. At this time, we are unable to move forward with your application. Best of luck in your job search.

Human Resources at Company name

After an in-person meeting

We enjoyed meeting with you and exploring your background. At this time, we will not be moving forward with your application. Best of luck in your job search.

Sign with the name of the person they met

Offer Letters

An organization is not obligated to provide a formal offer letter. However, providing one does give clarity of the offer presented and confidence to the candidate they have secured the position. This is especially important to candidates when they are leaving a current position to join your organization. An offer letter will also indicate any verbal conditions in writing should a dispute arise in the future.

Offer letters should be short and to the point. Key components will include:

- <u>Position being offered</u> – state the job title. Do not state the name of the supervisor, that is subject to change at any time.

- <u>Rate of pay</u> – stated by per pay period or hourly. Never state only annual salary. The organization could be liable for the full amount if an employee leaves the company. Although, for salaried employees it is common to add a sentence that says "your salary is equivalent to $XX,XXX annually".

- <u>Number of pay periods</u> – provide information as to when employees are paid. Candidates can then understand how their annual rate will be paid.

- <u>Benefits</u> – be sure to state these are our current benefits; subject to change at management discretion. Consider a statement similar to "you are eligible for benefits being offered to employees at this time, see attached benefit overview". Explaining the benefits in detail could create issues as they change over the years.

- <u>Start Date</u> – this can be negotiated, but they know you hope not to wait longer than the date that is stated.

- <u>Date the offer will expire</u> – if offer letter is not returned signed; you don't want them coming back in 3 months and saying I'm ready.

- <u>Employment-at-will language</u> – be sure this is consistent with your state law, but it is generally acceptable to state that employees may be terminated, or quit, at any time with or without notice.

- <u>Contingencies</u> – State if the offer is contingent upon completion of a background check, drug test and/or eligibility to work in the United States.

- <u>Signature of employer</u> and date signed

- <u>Signature of candidate</u> and date of acceptance

A sample for use is provided on the next page.

Sample Offer Letter

Candidate Name

Date

Delivered Via Email (if appropriate)

Dear CANDIDATE NAME,

We are excited to offer you the position of (insert position) beginning (hire date). Your pay will be based on ($$$) per pay period. At this time, we are issued pay checks every other week, for a total of 26 pay periods per year. That equates to an annual salary of ($$$) to be paid over the time you work.

Our current benefit package includes Medical, Dental, Vision, Retirement (include others you might offer.). You will be eligible for all benefits offered to other employees based on eligibility. We have provided the current benefit offering as an attachment. Understand that these subject to change during your employment.

If appropriate: Your offer is subject to positive completion of our background check process and drug testing process.

At all times, your employment will be on an at-will basis. This means you can resign at any time, and the company may end your employment with or without notice.

You will be asked to complete an I-9 form demonstrating your eligibility for work in the United States your first day of work. Your employment is contingent on successful completion of this document by law.

Welcome to (Company Name)!

Manager/Owner/HR

To accept our offer, please sign below and return no later than (date)

_____   _____
(Candidate's Name)   (date)

Action Items for recruiting in your organization:

1.	Ensure job descriptions exist and reflect current requirements

2.	Select applicable resources for marketing your positions

3.	Train managers on the recruiting process

4.	Consider candidate communication and add/revise as needed

5.	Create behavioral interview questions to be used throughout the organization

6.	Evaluate your interview process

7.	Create or revise offer letters

Chapter 4 — New Employee Orientation

The best recruiting strategy any organization can have is to retain top talent and minimize unplanned turnover. Think strategically to establish a long-term plan that will ensure your top talent is retained and those that are not adding value are terminated. In this section, we will look at how you can accomplish that initial relationship with the new hire orientation.

Retaining top talent starts on the first day of work. Consider engaging your new hires even earlier, before they start work, with a welcome phone call from their manager or peer. Properly introducing and assimilating new employees into your organization will have a positive impact on their performance and engagement for years to come.

Consider these five main objectives of new employee orientation. Each aspect is critical, but that doesn't mean it should be completed during their first few hours at your organization. Utilize these activities and action steps as touch points with your new hires over the first 60 days of employment.

Pieces of this process can be assigned to various members of your team to allow for interactions and introductions. Spreading the activities out during the first few months will allow touch points to be sure your new hire is assimilating into the organization. This also provides the new hire with an avenue for conversation about issues and skills they may be struggling with.

On the pages that follow you will find detailed activities for the first few months along with an orientation checklist that can be used to ensure all steps are covered.

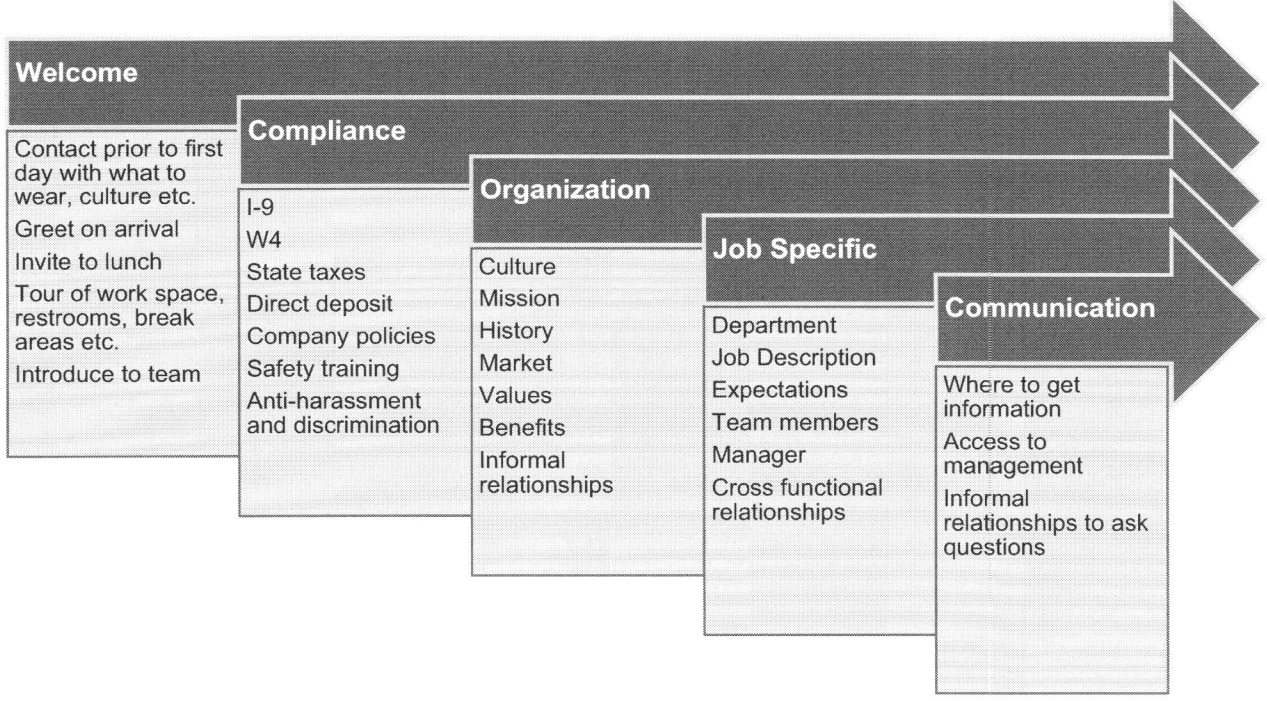

Sample Orientation Schedule

Prior to day one – Prepare for new hire

- **Set up workspace** – this should include basic supplies that will be needed on the first few days.

- **Create phone extension and email address** – have ready for the new hire immediately. Update internal company lists so employee is part of communication chain.

- **Send email to team notifying of new hire** – provide basic, non-confidential, information and start date with expectation that new hire will be welcomed immediately.

- **Contact Vendors** – if new hire will interact with others outside the organization provide information about role, start date and contact information.

- **Create training schedule** – determine what training is necessary and prepare others to be available.

First day – schedule time with manager and team members to ensure availability

- **Welcome** – Be sure a manager or team member is available to meet the new hire upon arrival and show them to their work area.

- **Facility tour and introductions** – In addition to meeting team members, be sure to point out the informal areas of the operation including vending machines, break areas, rest rooms etc.

- **Paperwork** – Determine what is essential to be completed quickly and provide time and direction for that to occur. This is typically payroll information, completion of I-9 form, access to the building or work area and benefit paperwork (only if benefits start within first 30 days).

- **Job description** – Managers should have created an appointment on their calendar to meet with the new employee and discuss job duties and expectations. Goals and performance standards that apply generically to the function should be discussed.

- **Skill review** – Employees are rarely hired with every skill needed to do the job. Ask the employee if they are aware of specific training they need quickly and provide assurance you will arrange the training.

- **Department procedures** – There are likely processes that will need to be complied with immediately such as how to record time worked, calling in sick, and safety procedures.

- **Questions** – Be open and encourage employees to ask questions. Remind them they won't remember everything, so feel free to come back and clarify or get direction as needed.

- **Create a deliverable assignment** – Employees want to be involved as soon as they arrive, and will retain information by doing "real" work. The assignment can be simple but productive, such as go through previous work, look for errors and make suggestions for how things might be done in the future.

- **Lunch** – Communicate the culture of breaks and meals early. If employees typically go out for lunch, be sure the manager or co-worker invites the new employee out the first day. If people typically stay in the office for meals, be sure the new hire is invited to join co-workers.

- **End of the work day** – Check in to see how things went. Let the employee know that you are excited they have joined the organization, and they are free to leave when their work is done, or at the designated time. Review the time people generally arrive the next day and that you'll look forward to seeing them then.

Second day

Check in to see what is still open from the day before. Ask the employee if anything came up they would like help with. Partner them with a team member they may not have met to learn a new part of their job. Allow them some independence to determine their own needs.

End of the first week

Expect your new hire to start blending in. They should be part of a group or team working on projects to assimilate into the department. All necessary paperwork should be completed and they should be comfortable in your facility. Allow some time to sit and talk casually. Ask how they feel about the position and the organization and provide very high level feedback. Find 2-3 positive things to say about their accomplishments. If there are skills that need work, mention in a way that shows you want to help.

After two weeks

A meeting should occur with the manager. Discuss how the employee is doing with job requirements. Check in regarding:

- ✓ Are they comfortable handling basic situations on their own?

- ✓ Do they feel they are lacking training on portions of the position?

Be open to situations and react positively about solutions.

30 – 60 days after start

At this point your employee should be comfortable with the position and their co-workers. Consider more informal check-ins to be sure you aren't missing anything. Consider exploring these areas with your new hire:

- ✓ Is there anything about the culture they would like to discuss?

- ✓ How is this position differing from their past role? Is that good or a challenge?

- ✓ Have they found additional training needs that may not have been discussed when they started?

- ✓ Do they feel welcome and a part of the work team?

- ✓ Are all the tools they need to do the job provided?

- ✓ What else might they like from you, their manager?

At the end of 30 and 60 days, provide open and honest feedback. If there are concerns about retention, share them now so there are no surprises.

New Hire Documentation

In the compliance section, we provided the full scope of an employee file. Many of the documents will be completed within the first few days of work. To ensure you collect all necessary documentation and consistently provide information to employees, have a standard orientation checklist. Templates are provided on the following pages for most of the items discussed – but be sure to customize these for the areas of specific need in your organization.

All employees should complete:

- I-9 form – electronically or a current form issued by the Department of Homeland Security. This MUST be completed by the employee and the organization within 72 hours of starting work. Always be sure you are using a current form for new hires.

- Employment application – if not completed and signed during the hiring process, complete now. The application shown in the recruiting section will provide assurance that information gathered is accurate and your new hire understands the employment arrangement.

- Tax deduction forms – The Federal W4 is required for all. Most states have a corresponding W4 for withholding purposes. Your local municipality might also have tax withholding requirements as well. Check with your payroll vendor or state department of labor if you are unsure of your obligations.

- Direct deposit form – Employees must provide authorization for you to access their bank account. Having a copy of a check is helpful to insure proper data entry, but the form must also be on file as well.

- Acceptance of tools – Consider using this form for anything you give employees including access card, keys etc. It becomes especially important when there are items of high value such as computer, mobile phone etc.

- Post offer medical information – Workers compensation claims are increasingly becoming an issue for all employers. By collecting baseline information at the time of hire, you have a defense in the future about claims that might be made. Once completed, this form MUST be retained in a separate location from the employee file. For small organizations, a binder or folder similar to I-9 retention is sufficient.

- Other forms used in many organizations might include:

  - Emergency contacts

  - Benefit information required by your vendors

  - Uniform, tools or equipment provided agreement

  - Employee handbook receipt

  - Safety documents needed by your industry

New Hire Orientation Checklist

This is a sample of common discussions and paperwork completed in the first few days with a new hire. Do not overload the employee with complex information on their first day. Some items, such as specifics of the benefit program, can wait until the actual time of enrollment.

The form should be customized to the needs and culture of your organization.

Name:		Hire Date:	

Documents

☐ I-9	☐ Federal W-4	☐ State W-4	☐ Direct deposit
☐ Driver's License (if applicable)	☐ Emergency contact	☐ Signed application	☐ Signed offer letter

Introduction and Socialization

☐ Tour of facility	☐ Introduction to team	☐ Workspace	☐ Restrooms
☐ Telephone	☐ Parking	☐ Office Supplies	☐ Break area
☐ Work schedule	☐ Payroll practices	☐ Contact points for questions	

Position specific needs

☐ Job Description	☐ Computer	☐ Access to work space (keys, cards etc.)	
☐ Email	☐ Required passwords	☐ Office supplies	

Compensation and Benefits

☐ Confirm starting salary	☐ Overtime rules	☐ Reporting of time	☐ Check date
☐ Overview of benefits	☐ Paid time off	☐ Holidays	☐ Access to systems

Policies and Procedures

☐ Employee handbook	☐ Signed acknowledgement	

Review key policies:

☐ Mission of company	☐ Organizational overview (location, products etc.)		
☐ Anti-harassment	☐ Use of technology	☐ Attendance	
☐ Requesting time off	☐ Smoking	☐ Confidentiality	
☐ Safety	☐ FMLA (if applicable)	☐ Dress Code	

Employee Signature:		Date:	

Payroll/HR New Hire Payroll Entry

The first few days of an employee's orientation are filled with paperwork. Be sure all documents are collected and completed in their entirety. Keep this form out and available until all is completed. Then file all in payroll system or employee file together.

Employee Name: _____   **Hire Date**: _____

Job Title: _____   **Starting Wage**: _____ per (hour) (year)

Employee sent new hire welcome including forms:

_____

State Withholding: _____   **New State Needed**: ☐ Yes ☐ No

Documents to be retained:

Document	Received	Completed	Notes
Resume			
Application			
Offer Letter			
I-9			
W4 - Fed			
W4 - State			
Direct Deposit			
Handbook Acknowledgement			
Benefits Enrollment			
Equipment receipt			

Documents for new hire:

Employee self-service how to information			
Temporary benefit ID cards			
Initial COBRA notification			
Instructions on phone/internet			
Necessary ID, Keys etc			

Payroll Change Notice

Date _____   Department _____

Employee Name _____   Title _____

Effective Date: _____

Check Appropriate Box for Action to be taken:

☐ Add to Payroll   ☐ Change Withholding Rate *(Complete new W-4 form)*

☐ Change Rate   New Rate: _____ per _____

☐ Change Status to: ☐ Full-Time ☐ Part-Time ☐ Temporary

☐ Remove from Payroll

☐ Change Title/Classification to: _____

☐ Leave of Absence: Paid?   ☐ Yes ☐ No

Return (*Anticipated Date of Return*) _____

☐ Transfer to: (Department)_____   ☐ Change of Shift_____

☐ Address/Information Change   _____

_____

Reason for Payroll Change:

☐ Merit Increase   ☐ See Performance Appraisal   ☐ New Employee

☐ Promotion   ☐ Other/Bonus _____

Reason for Separation:

☐ Voluntary   ☐ Discharged   ☐ Laid Off   ☐ Other

Comments: _____

_____

_____

Submitted By: _____ Title: _____Date: _____

Approved By: _____ Title: _____Date: _____

I-9 Completion Process

Complete I-9
- Be sure you're using the most recent form for new hires
- Must be completed after offer, but before first 72 hours of work
- Review documents and records, retain copies of valid documents if that aligns with your policy
- Employees can select any documents to bring that are listed

Retain for all employees
- You must have an I-9 for all working employees after November 1986
- File in a I-9 file, not employee files. Generally a 3 ring binder is fine
- Create a notification system of eligibility documents with expiration dates

Upon Seperation
- Retain I-9's for the LONGER of:
- 3 years from date or hire OR
- 1 year from date of separation

Annually
- Audit I-9s for accuracy and completeness
- Move those employees that are no longer required out of the file
- Update any documents that are expiring soon

To keep copies or not……..

This is a common question on the I-9s. There is no legal obligation to retain copies. However, without copies it is difficult to audit your I-9 forms in the future. On the flip side, with the increase of identity theft, there is risk in retaining copies in your office. If you are unsure which is the right choice for your organization, discuss with your legal counsel.

Direct Deposit Form

I authorize _____ to initiate automatic deposits into my account at the financial institution(s) listed below. I also authorize the same company to make withdrawals from this account in the event that a credit entry is due.

Further, I agree not to hold the company responsible for any delay or loss of funds due to incorrect or incomplete information supplied by me or my financial institution. This includes any error on the part of my financial institution in depositing funds to my account.

This agreement will remain in effect until I provide the company with a written notice of cancellation from me or my financial institution. I may submit a new direct deposit form to the payroll function at any time and request a change to the information below.

I understand that the initial direct deposit may take up to 2 payroll cycles to begin. During that time, my banking information may be tested to ensure accuracy and I will be provided my wages due in the form of a traditional check.

Name of Institution	Bank Routing Number	Account Number	Checking or savings account	Amount to be deposited or Net for full amount

To insure accuracy, please attach a copy of a voided check or instructions from your bank.

Employee Name: _____

Employee Signature: _____   Date: _____

Acceptance of Equipment, Tools and Resources

Name:_____

Below is an ongoing list of the items received during employment for which I am responsible. I agree to return all items in usable condition, given normal wear and tear, no later than when I separate my employment. If I fail to do so, I give permission for the company to deduct the amount shown from my final paycheck; as allowed by law.

Item	Value	Date Received	Employee Initials	Date Returned	Employee and company initials

Employee Signature _____ Date _____

Company Signature _____ Date: _____

Post-Job Offer Medical Questionnaire

Employee Name: _____   Date of Birth: _____/_____/_____

Height: _____   Weight: _____   Date Completed: _____/_____/_____

EMPLOYEE AFFIRMATION: I herewith affirm that the employer has made me an offer of employment, conditioned on, among other things, the satisfactory completion of this questionnaire. The purpose of this inquiry is as follows: (1) to determine whether I currently have the physical qualifications necessary to perform the essential functions of the job that has been offered; (2) to determine what accommodations, if any, may be necessary for me to perform the essential functions of the job; and (3) to determine whether I can perform the essential functions of the job without posing a significant direct threat to the health and safety of myself and others. This information will be kept strictly confidential in a separate medical file, apart from my personnel file. I hereby affirm that the questions in the medical questionnaire have not been asked of me by anyone with the employer until after I have signed this statement and been offered a conditional job. The conditional job duties have been adequately described to me, and I have had an opportunity to ask questions regarding the duties.

GINA DISCLOSURE: The Genetic Information Nondiscrimination Act of 2008 (GINA) prohibits employers from requesting or requiring genetic information of an individual or family member of the individual, except as specifically allowed by law. To comply with this law, we are asking that you not provide any genetic information when responding to this request for medical information. "Genetic information" includes an individual's family medical history, the results of an individual's or family member's genetic tests, the fact that an individual or an individual's family member sought or received genetic services, and genetic information of a fetus carried by an individual or an individual's family member or an embryo lawfully held by an individual or family member receiving assistive reproductive services.

1.   Have you ever had or been treated for any of the following conditions or diseases?

	YES	NO		YES	NO
Herniated Disc	☐	☐	Arm/hand injury	☐	☐
Knee injury	☐	☐	Wrist problems, including Carpal Tunnel Syndrome	☐	☐
Surgical removal of disc or spinal fusion	☐	☐	Repetitive motion disorders	☐	☐
Back injury	☐	☐	Broken bones	☐	☐
Hernia or rupture	☐	☐	Ankylosis (immobility) of any major, weight-bearing joints (ankles, knees, hips)	☐	☐
Diseased process of the spine	☐	☐	Tendonitis	☐	☐
Neck injury, pain or problems	☐	☐	Head injury	☐	☐
Chest Pain	☐	☐	Amputations	☐	☐
Shoulder injury	☐	☐	Epilepsy, fainting spells, or dizziness	☐	☐
Arthritis or rheumatism	☐	☐	Compressed air sequelae (damage to lungs, ruptured ear drum, etc due to explosion, air concussion, etc.)	☐	☐
Do you have partial loss of hearing?	☐	☐	Have you ever had an audiogram (hearing test)?	☐	☐
Do you need glasses to read or for distance?	☐	☐	Any serious injuries?	☐	☐
Surgery?	☐	☐	High blood pressure?	☐	☐
Ever refused surgery?	☐	☐			

Please explain if your answer is YES to any of the above questions:

_____

_____

_____

2. **Have you sought treatment from a healthcare provider for any of the above injuries and/or medical conditions?** .... ☐ YES ☐ NO

If Yes, please explain: _____

3. **Have you received a copy of the job description for your position?** .... ☐ YES ☐ NO

If No, please stop here and request one.

4. **Are you capable of performing the essential duties of this job function?** .... ☐ YES ☐ NO

If Yes, please explain: _____

5. **Do you have any injury or condition that requires a reasonable accommodation in order for you to be able to perform the essential duties of this job position?** .... ☐ YES ☐ NO

If "YES", what accommodations do you need to perform the job?

_____

_____

_____

6. **How much weight can you lift comfortably unassisted?**

☐ < 15 lbs   ☐ 15-25 lbs   ☐ 25-39 lbs   ☐ ≥ 40 lbs

7. **Has a healthcare provider placed any limitations on your ability to sit, stand, push, pull, or lift?**
.... ☐ YES ☐ NO

If "YES", what are the limitations?

_____

_____

_____

8. **Has a healthcare provider limited the amount of weight you can lift?** .... ☐ YES ☐ NO

If "YES", list the weight limitation and the date that your healthcare provider issued you the limitation?

_____

_____

_____

9. **Are you taking any prescribed drugs that would interfere with your ability to safely perform your job?**
.... ☐ YES ☐ NO

If yes, please list the medications.

_____

_____

_____

My signature certifies that all facts and representations made by me are true, accurate and made willingly and intentionally.

_____   _____   _____
Signature   Print Your Name   Date

_____   _____
Company Representative   Date

Action Items for new employee integration in your organization:

1.	**Formalize our New Hire Orientation process**
2.	**Train/talk to team about importance of new hires**
3.	**Customize New Hire Checklist**
4.	**Implement Acceptance of Tools and Post Offer Medical documentation**

Chapter 5 — Employee Alignment and Engagement

We all talk about performance management in human resources; however, the question being asked today ... *is performance yours to manage*? You need employees who are effective and engaged. As adults, we hope they will take responsibility for that. Unfortunately, that isn't always the case.

Productivity and alignment with goals are two of the most important processes at your organization. When feedback is provided effectively, employees will see the link between what they do and what you need to be successful. They will understand what needs to be done, and how it impacts the whole organization.

Studies indicate that the employee in the workforce today does not want their *performance managed* but are craving feedback. Employee feedback has a very real place in your organization. It will impact:

- How employees align their actions with goals
- Compliance obligations
- Engaging the employee
- Planning for the future
- Supporting your employees desire to do a great job
- Understand how they fit into the overall organization

Therefore, the focus today is moving toward more frequent conversational feedback sessions and a limited reliance on formal documentation. Ideally, a monthly sit down with the manager and employee will serve your organization well. While it can seem overwhelming to meet with employees monthly, quarterly is generally workable for most managers and will still provide an acceptable level of engagement with your team.

Consider the real reason you are meeting with an employee each time the conversations occur. You are using valuable organizational resources with each meeting, so be clear on the purpose. The meeting might be to:

- Set or review goals
- Discuss salary
- Confirm that the employee understands the business goals
- Provide feedback
- Spend time with the employee to show you care
- Compliance

OR all the above!

On the next page, you will see a simple form that might guide this type of conversation. We would recommend setting up a workbook for each employee and then update as each conversation occurs. A sample Excel workbook can be found on the toolkit website. Set appointments for the year in your calendar and invite the employee to make sure they happen. The date and time can move if needed during the year, but without the system in place, they are likely to be forgotten.

Topic	Notes during or following the meeting
Successes this month	
Challenges to be solved	
Progress toward goals	
Training/tools needed	
Other	

Annual documentation is still recommended, although not intended to be the focus of the meetings. For your annual review, consider a document that gives a broad overview of the past year, but primarily focuses the conversation toward the new year. The meeting should discuss goals, training and the next steps for the employee in your organization.

The timing of this review is based on organizational convenience. Businesses may choose to complete annual reviews throughout the year, for example on an employee's anniversary. Others decide it's best to have all reviews at the same time to ensure alignment with ever changing goals and the budget setting process for the new year. Either system works – just be sure it's done!

Some tips for a systematic program of employee engagement and feedback should include:

- Be prepared for the conversation, have notes, and plan the time and place.
- Give the employee notice in advance of the meeting.
- Provide the written document a few hours in advance to allow the employee time to read the document in advance.
- Always focus on high level accomplishments and opportunities for improvement. Handle the "nitty gritty" during the monthly check-in meetings.
- When constructive feedback is required, be very specific and give examples where possible.
- Describe expected behaviors and provide examples of how to achieve them.
- Get the employees feedback and allow them to participate in the meeting.
- Train managers and employees to give and receive feedback in a positive and productive way.

Performance alignment will always be extremely customized for each organization. The system must fit the culture, employee population and compliance needs of each team. While it is difficult to provide a one size fits all document, you will find the documents on the next few pages can be customized and used as a starting point for your organization.

Annual Review Process

Below we outline a typical performance alignment process and the action items that would fall under each. Then we provide a sample of performance management documents that can be adapted and utilized in your organization.

Prior to the Meeting

- Focus on performance for the entire review period
- Consider opportunities in the organization this employee might qualify for
- Give employee notice so that he/she can prepare for the discussion
- Review any previous communication about performance
- Avoid considering some aspects of the job at the expense of others
- Review job description against performance
- Schedule meeting and reserve private space

Discussion of Appraisal

- Provide copy of written review 2 – 4 hours before the meeting
- Begin the discussion by creating a sincere, open and friendly atmosphere
- Let employee know this is intended to be a conversation and their input is important to the process
- Explain the agenda for the meeting
- Review the job description together – is it still an accurate reflection of the position
- Discuss the following – be sure to describe the behaviors, don't judge
  - Employee's strengths
  - Areas for growth in the performance categories
  - Significant accomplishments from the past period
  - Ways to improve performance
  - Barriers to effective work performance and job satisfaction
  - Employee's goals and needs for development
- Allow the employee to provide feedback and suggestions for supervisor
- Discuss anything else the employee or supervisor would like to address
- Complete appraisal forms, as applicable
- When speaking with the employee, try not to:
  - Be critical of personalities or try to change them
  - Avoid or skate around difficult discussions
  - Do all the talking – the best reviews are a two-way street
  - Force change on an employee that may not be interested

The Follow-Up

- Immediately after the meeting record the plans made and points requiring follow-up
- Provide a copy of any written documentation for the employee
- Review goals quarterly to ensure you stay on track

Performance Review Forms

Personal Contribution Thoughts (to be completed by the employee and provided to manager approximately one week prior to the review)

Your company name and logo

Name:		Date:	

How have I contributed to the operational mission, goals, and stakeholders?

Where do I wish I could have contributed but didn't? Why?

New learning or skills I have acquired, relationships I've built to make me (or our group) more productive.

My strengths:

What I want to be doing next year and 3-5 years from now.

I would like to develop the following skill sets:

In order to be most successful, I need more support in the following areas:

Please tell us how you feel your job description reflects your current responsibilities:

Contribution Overview

Your company name and logo

The categories should reflect the mission and initiatives in your organization. Use this as a template to customize and initiate a conversation with your employees that will emphasize your goals and align their performance.

EMPLOYEE INFORMATION	
Employee Name	Job Title

Review Period

From: / /   To: / /   Manager:

Performance Category	Rating	Results and Impact of actions
Knowledge of Position: *Possesses required skills, knowledge, and abilities to competently perform the job. Understands what needs to be done and completes job description tasks.*	☐ Outstanding ☐ Expected Performance ☐ Improvement Needed ☐ Developing	
Quality of Work: *Work is completed accurately (few or no errors), efficiently and within deadlines with appropriate level of supervision. Asks questions as expected and makes decisions that are appropriate for level of responsibility and experience.*	☐ Outstanding ☐ Expected Performance ☐ Improvement Needed ☐ Developing	
Collaboration: *Respectful of colleagues, participants, parents and stakeholders. Looks for input from others as appropriate. Makes valuable contributions to help the group achieve its strategic goals*	☐ Outstanding ☐ Expected Performance ☐ Improvement Needed ☐ Developing	
Initiative & Flexibility: *Takes responsibility for completing tasks and seeks out additional responsibility. Identifies problems and solution. Eager to take on new challenges. Adjusts to unexpected changes as expected.*	☐ Outstanding ☐ Expected Performance ☐ Improvement Needed ☐ Developing	
Vision and Purpose: *Effectively embraces our vision and sense of core purpose. Keeps goals of organization front of mind in all decision making. Supports mission through attendance at events and giving.*	☐ Outstanding ☐ Expected Performance ☐ Improvement Needed ☐ Developing	

Priority Setting: *Understands what is critical and what can delay based on competing requests. Uses time effectively and can identify and eliminate road-blocks that may hinder projects.*	☐ Outstanding ☐ Expected Performance ☐ Improvement Needed ☐ Developing	
Lifelong learning: *Continually seeks ways to strengthen performance; cross trains in other areas; and regularly monitors new developments in field of work*	☐ Outstanding ☐ Expected Performance ☐ Improvement Needed ☐ Developing	

Overall Analysis

☐ **Ready for additional responsibilities** *Employee excels in position; exceeds expectations in most areas and is working on new skills in others. Consider goals to increase level of responsibility and engagement.*	☐ **Excellent Team member** *Employee satisfies all essential job requirements; exceeds expectations in some areas and is working improving in others. Very happy to have as a member of the team.*	☐ **Developing** *Employee is working at the level of someone learning or perfecting this position. The progress is as anticipated and future development is within reach.*

We count on you for:

Opportunities for future skill building:

FUTURE PLANS

Goal	Measurable Outcome	Anticipated Completion	Comments

Training Requests/Opportunities for the year:

Additional Employee Comments:

Acknowledgement

I acknowledge that I have had the opportunity to discuss this overview with my manager/ supervisor and I have received a copy of the written notes.

Employee Signature: Date:

Reviewer Signature: Date:

Goal Setting

Goals are the foundation of any forward-thinking performance alignment process. To be effective, the employee should have control and accountability for the success or failure of attaining the goal. The manager should feel confident that by providing an objective measurable goal, the next performance alignment meeting will produce results.

There are five steps to effective goal setting which create the SMART acronym:

Specific – Clearly state WHAT is to be accomplished and for whom.

Measurable – How will the end results be measured. Use quantitative measures of cost, quality or time, whenever possible.

Action-oriented – Emphasize the need to take a specific action to achieve desired results.

Realistic – Ask the employee to stretch their current abilities, but ensure the goal is within reach and will not be so difficult to attain that it becomes frustrating.

Time Bound – When is the goal expected to be achieved?

S	M	A	R	T
Specific	Measurable	Action-Oriented	Realistic	Time Bound

Specific accomplishment	How will it be measured	What action steps need to be taken?	Is this realistic to expect you to complete? What do you need from the company?	When can we expect this to be finished? Should there be interim completion steps?	Additional Thoughts: Who do you need help from? Is a budget needed for training or completion?

Identifying and Retaining Top Talent

The task of retaining top talent should be the responsibility of all team members. When creating a plan for retention of employees, step one is to identify your top talent. Turnover can be productive for the organization to bring in new ideas and provide promotion opportunities. The key is for you to know who you want to retain, and who might fall into the category of acceptable turnover. Later in the section we'll address the unpleasant reality of employees who are not top talent!

Employees who fit into the top talent category are not necessarily the people who have been around the longest or have a relationship with the customer you think you can't live without. They are the people who have the work ethic and institutional knowledge that would put your organization at a disadvantage if you lost them. Top talent refers to the people you want on your team in twenty years and in whom you are willing to invest the time and resources to get them where they need to be to serve the organization in the future.

All organizations should identify top talent as approximately 2-3% of the employee population. These are not necessarily people in management today, but the team members that you are counting on to drive the business forward 20 years from today. They may never become management, but are still a critical component of your success. Remember, too many chiefs can be a problem – consider top talent across the organization by engaging those that will follow with precise and committed engagement.

It is valuable to keep an eye on this group and ensure you are providing opportunities for advancement, connection to the mission of the organization, and support for their personal growth and development. You don't want a situation where you spend three years grooming top talent, only to find they have gone to your competitor because they offer better health insurance. Understand what motivates your top talent and provide that for them. Consider the diagram on the next page, and use the worksheet that follows to identify the employees you would put into this important category.

©HR Topics 2020

	Ambition	Performance	Potential	Behavior	Engagement	Talent
	Exhibits passion for goals and success	Current performance is outstanding	Possess the soft skills needed for success	Actions fit the culture of the organization	Asks questions, meets goals, understands your mission	Has the innate ability to meet the demands of growth
Employee 1						
Employee 2						
Employee 3						

Engaging Employees

We spend more time with our co-workers than we do with the people we choose to spend our life with. But we don't get a choice in who our co-workers are. It's for this reason that employee engagement is a priority today. This is not a new concept. We've had company picnics, holiday parties and monthly gatherings for years in organizations. What has changed today is the way in which we engage employees.

What employees want are connections, personal and professional. Teambuilding activities can take on a wide variety of programming activities. Many of your planned engagement activities will have an obvious focus on business and productivity. That's fine, employees expect to see that connection. The goal is to provide a sense of community at the same time.

In addition to scheduled communication and activities, there are several technology platforms that can be used for informal relationship building. Employees are used to turning to social media to stay connected, and they want to have the same systems available at work. Consider those commonly available such as private Facebook or LinkedIn groups. This allows the more informal conversations about who is in the office, project progress, and general announcements about babies, weddings etc. that create connections.

You can't expect everyone to be best friends, but a certain degree of professionalism and comradery is a realistic expectation and one that is desired by your employees.

The goal of any engagement activity should be to elevate the mission of the company and remind employees "we're all in this together".

On the following page, you will find a sample employee engagement calendar. It is not management's responsibility to determine, plan or execute every event. A great way to get employees involved is to assign a month and theme to members of your team. Ask employees or groups to take charge of events. You will see in the attached chart we consider both business and wellness related topics. Think about what is important to your organization, and plan the events accordingly.

Engaging the top talent that you've identified

Who are they?

- Meet with the employee to confirm interest
- Let them know you consider them top talent
- Ask if they feel engaged and appreciated
- What are they looking for from the organization
- Where would they like to be in 5 or 10 years

Engaging Top Talent

- Set short and long term goals
- What training is available
- Engage the employee in your industry
- Attend national conference
- Participate in industry committee
- Visit vendors and customers
- Participation in internal events
- Attend management meetings

Retaining them

- One-on-one meetings with management
- Invite top talent to social events
- Customize available resources
- Responsibility for project team
- Presentation to management or employees
- Mentor others
- Define career path
- Provide bonus opportunities

Employee Engagement and Wellness Calendar

Connecting employees throughout the organization and with leadership is a key to employee engagement. This is very effective when the group is brought together through events and meetings in the organization. Use this sample monthly calendar to generate ideas and programs that would be relevant within your organization. It is especially effective to assign a committee of employees to be responsible for the communication and programming.

	Business programming	Employee wellness
January	Lunch and Learn Industry related topic, possibly outside speaker or vendor	Introduction to resources in the neighborhood for exercise, nutrition, doctors etc.
February	Respect in the workplace – could be team led or outside expert	Bring in specialist on lifting for a conversation – maybe a chiropractor
March	Technology – using apps on your phone? Personal growth topic	Contest of self-reported steps taken – distances from office around your area as goals
April	Lunch and Learn – financial management	Personal trainer to show exercises that can be done at your workspace
May	Business update and industry news for remainder of year	Celebrating the woman in your life that made a difference – tie into Mother's Day
June	Open house at facility for employee families	Walks at lunch every week
July	Lunch and Learn – Stress Management	Outdoor BBQ with healthy options and recipes
August	Tour of various departments allowing employees to present to one another	Water balloon toss outside; contest by department
September	Technology topic related to your business activities	Therapist to discuss difficult conversations and confrontation
October	Lunch and Learn – Business related topic	Cooking class – healthy eating
November	Thanksgiving – thank you for each other and a great year	Nutritionist to talk about eating during holidays!
December	Holiday celebration; Pot luck lunch with recipes provided	Indoor exercise call together

Training Alternatives

Get creative with how to provide development opportunities for your top talent. The traditional training class or conference is great, but there are a number of avenues that are all very good. Employees learn in many ways, and often the most effective growth comes from trying new skills.

Beyond traditional training

Modification of Current Job

- New Responsibilities
- Increased Span of Control
- Exposure to Other Functions and Roles
- Participation on Special Projects

Self-Directed Development

- Reading Materials
- Research Articles
- Professional Networks
- On-line Work Communities

External Experiences

- Community Activities
- External Networking
- Professional Associations
- Speaking Engagements
- Executive Directorships

Stretch Assignments

- Increase in Scope
- Stretch Project Assignment
- Organization-wide Committee
- Team Leadership Assignment
- Increased Visibility to Senior Management

Individualized Feedback

- Individual Assessment
- 360 Feedback
- Individual Coaching
- Structured Mentoring

Learning Events

- Training Programs
- Career Development Courses
- Seminars and Workshops
- On Line Education
- Certification Programs

Implementing these programs will require a budget for employee training and development. Employees should understand what the organization is willing to pay for, and what they might be expected to contribute, even if only their own time. Best practice would suggest that training should have some impact on performance and organizational success.

On the following page, a template is created to draft your own training and development policy. Consider how this can be incorporated into your organization. An overview should be shared with employees and added to your employee handbook.

Employee Training and Development Sample Process

Our company supports the growth and development of our team. We provide the opportunity for you to move your career forward by recognizing that you may be in need of financial assistance or flexible work arrangements to continue your education.

This form should be given to your manager PRIOR to your registering for a course or program. Only then are we able to discuss our ability to assist. Should you start a course, there is no guarantee that we will meet your needs. At all times, you must be able to complete the essential functions of your position at a performance level that is acceptable to the organization.

Note to business: Consider eligibility that provides higher reimbursement to those with longer tenure. For example:

Years of Service	Maximum benefit per year full time employees. *Part time employees entitled to pro-rated share*
1 – 5	$1,500
6 – 10	$2,250
11+	$3,500

Eligibility:

- Employee of organization for a minimum of 1 year prior to the course start date; continued employment throughout course/program

- Performance review rating that demonstrates you meet or exceed our expectations

- Not have any current performance issues or concerns from your manager

- Courses must be offered from approved institutions

- Connection to current role or future development within our organization

Expectation of participation:

- Regular attendance at all meetings

- Share knowledge with team, department or organization

- Promote organization within the activity (for examples, business cards, logo attire)

- Receive grade of C or higher, or pass if pass/fail course

Included expenses:

- Required materials

- Meals if part of event/meeting

- For networking/industry events travel required outside of normal travel to work

Form to request training payment or reimbursement

Name: _____   Date of Hire:_____

Program requested: _____

Type of program:

☐   Seminar – single date
☐   Seminar – multiple sessions
☐   Conference
☐   Degree level coursework
      ☐ Associates   ☐ Bachelors   ☐ Graduate
☐   Ongoing membership

Details about program and institution:

Program offered by: _____

Start Date: _____   Length of program: _____

Request is for: $ _____

Details of fee requested:

Cost of program/class: _____

Necessary Tools/Books: _____

Travel: _____

Misc: _____

Details of time off from work requested: _____

This will benefit my current or future role in what way?

_____

_____

Approvals:

Amount Approved: _____   Time off Approved: _____

Approved by immediate supervisor: _____   Date:_____

Approved by HR or Leader: _____   Date:_____

I understand that I must remain in good standing with the company. If I am no longer employed during the program, or within 6 months of completion, the cost of the program will be taken from my final paycheck.

Employee Signature upon approval: _____   Date:_____

And When It's Just Not Working....

There are those employees that will never be top talent, and no matter how hard you try you just can't get them on your page.

Unfortunately, not all feedback is positive. When issues arise with regard to performance, it is critical that you address it immediately. Your goal is to identify any job-related issues as early as possible and coach the employee to improve. If you have concerns about an employee's performance, you need to discuss those concerns with the employee immediately. With immediate feedback, employees can improve, and if they don't improve, your decision to change the employment relationship should not come as a surprise.

Leaders must be willing to terminate poor performers. While it will always be the worst part of a management role, retaining employees that are not productive will pull down the productivity of the entire team. After constructive conversation and training, the decision may have to be made to terminate the employee.

Consider these steps for an effective meeting on performance alignment when a situation requires immediate change:

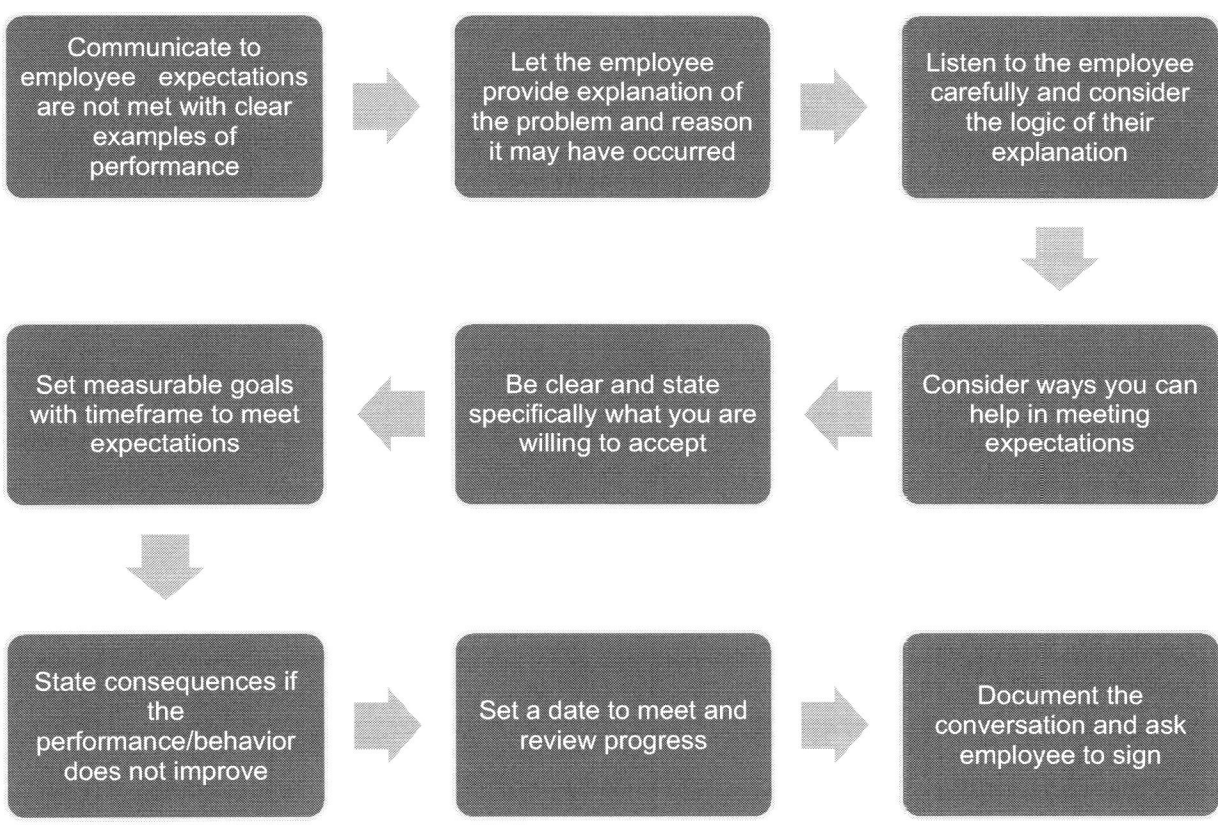

If performance does not change to your satisfaction, be prepared to meet the employee and formally document the situation. Use the following templates for formal documentation. You can either have the employee sign the document or send a copy via email for the employee's records. That will also create an electronic record for your files that the employee was notified of the situation.

Date:

To:

I noticed: _____ which was a problem because _____.

In the future, I expect you to _____
_____.

We agreed you will
_____ so we get back on track.

I will provide you with _____ to help be sure that happens.

Thanks for understanding.

Your Name

If the requested action is not fixed, write the employee a memo with the same language as above.

Add to the memo:
If this is not corrected immediately, the next step will be _____

Managers often say it's easier to live with the employee they know rather than start over. There is some truth to this. What we are certain of is that by allowing sub-standard performance to remain on your team, you are sending a message to all that it's acceptable to perform at that level.

As we think about separation, consider the chart on the next page. It is intended to help you understand the full cost of turnover. You may be surprised by the real cost to your organization. It is for this reason that we encourage you to recruit with care and retain the employees that impact your bottom line. The cost of unemployment is often discussed but does not have the financial impact to business that is often assumed.

Separation is a difficult moment for all. On the next pages, we provide a template for separation documentation. To guide through the process, you will find an exit interview and a worksheet to calculate the true cost of unemployment to your organization on the following pages.

Corrective Action Documentation

Name:		Date:	

The following issue is causing concern regarding your performance

This has caused......

In the future, we need you to.....

Indicate specific training or tools that will be used to correct this situation (if appropriate)

We will review the situation (state number of days if performance related)

Should this occur again in the future we will be forced to....

We appreciate your attention to this matter. Signatures below indicate the issue was discussed on the date indicated above.

_____
Manager Signature

_____
Employee Signature

Termination Letter

We often return to the adage: Less is More! In most circumstance, you are not obligated to put the termination issue in writing. However, it is often helpful at the final meeting to have a document prepared that an employee can take documenting the critical post-employment information.

State law is a critical component of the termination process. Be sure to check your State Department of Labor regulations for separation details and final pay requirements.

Be especially careful with **employees over the age of 40 if you are offering a severance**. The Older Workers Benefit Protection Act requires these employees are given time to consider the offer and provided a period to rescind acceptance even after the document is returned. For this reason, it is recommended you review the separation document of employees over the age of 40 with an attorney.

Severance pay is never required, but something many organizations choose to provide if a separation is occurring through no fault of their own. When severance is warranted, many organizations use a benchmark of 1-2 weeks of pay for every year of service. It is not uncommon to have a minimum of 4 weeks of severance, and then add a week per year for those with longer tenure. The amounts can vary but should be based on valid business decisions to eliminate any question regarding discrimination.

In the letter on the following page, you will find notes on typical areas that are included. The items that are underlined are those areas you need to consider before you simply cut and paste! Each letter will be fairly different based on the circumstances of separation and state law. Be sure to give thought to what you are putting in writing as the employee will have this forever.

Dear XXXXXX,

Your employment with (company name) will be ending on (last day of work). You will be paid through (date pay will end). This decision was made due to: (be specific and honest – or omit this line.)

Below is information that you might find helpful.

You will receive your final paycheck on: _____ (check state law for requirement)

> This will be direct deposited as usual: *Caution – if they have tools, keys, equipment etc. to return, consider stopping the direct deposit and have them pick up their check when they return the materials.*

Unemployment: We will or will not be contesting your unemployment. Please apply for determination of eligibility.

> *Some states require you provide an unemployment document* – check this.

Insurance: If you have over 20 employees you need to provide COBRA; under 20 employees you may have state regulations that come into play. If COBRA comes into play, state that you will receive COBRA information in the next 15 days. The company is responsible for the documentation, but check with your benefit broker if they, or the insurance company, can send on your behalf. If not, check state law and contact your insurance broker for proper language. If you are under 20 employees, follow state requirements.

Vacation/Sick/Paid Time Off – this depends on your policy and state law. Check to see what must be paid in your state and how it should be accrued under your policy. Also indicate when they will receive this payment.

Confidentiality, non-compete or non-disclosure agreement – if in place, please remember that you are bound by the signed agreement. We trust you will comply and no further discussion or action will be required.

References in the future – please direct any request for employment information to (insert contact name). We will be happy to provide basic employment information. You can also state if you are providing a letter of recommendation with the separation.

Address any questions you have after your departure to (insert contact name). Please be sure to keep us informed of any change to your personal information so we can send documents to you in the future, such as your W2. If you do not receive expected communication such as your W2 or Benefit paperwork, please contact us immediately.

We wish you the best of luck in the future,

Name _____

Title _____

Exit Checklist

Name:		Position:	
Supervisor:		Reason for Separation:	
Separation Date:		Last day worked:	

	Reviewed	**Forwarded to Proper Person**

Items to Review with employee

	Reviewed	Forwarded to Proper Person
State continuation or COBRA forms	☐	☐
Health/Dental – termination papers	☐	☐
Vacation time payable	☐	☐
Final Paycheck date: _____	☐	☐
Outstanding expenses: ☐ Yes ☐ No	☐	☐
Any bonus or commissions due	☐	☐
Unemployment Compensation	☐	☐
Advise on change of address for W2 and Benefits	☐	☐
Reminder of confidentiality provisions	☐	☐
Other: _____	☐	☐

Items to be Returned

	Reviewed	Forwarded to Proper Person
Keys	☐	☐
Credit Cards/Calling Cards	☐	☐
Cell phone/Pager	☐	☐
Tools provided by the company	☐	☐
Laptop or tablet	☐	☐
Other: _____	☐	☐

To be handled internally

Communication plan established internally and externally	☐ Completed
Eligible for Re-employment	☐ Yes ☐ No *Reason*: _____
Security code/company changed	☐ Completed
Access to systems removed	☐ Completed
Disable phone and delete voicemail	☐ Completed
Email forwarded; auto reply message set	☐ Completed
File paperwork or resignation in employee file	☐ Completed
Move employee file to terminated area if physical files	☐ Completed
Move I-9 to terminated file	☐ Completed

_____
Employee Signature

_____
Date

_____
Manager's Signature

_____
Date

Exit Interview Form

Name:		Date:	
Interviewer:		Supervisor:	
Position:		Department:	
Hire Date:		Termination Date:	

Please check how the following issues played into your decision to leave our company.

	Primary	Secondary
Secured a higher paying job	☐	☐
Secured a more interesting job	☐	☐
Leaving the workforce	☐	☐
Hours conflicting with other commitments	☐	☐
Issues with Supervisors	☐	☐
Disliked the work	☐	☐
Disliked the environment	☐	☐
Transportation problems	☐	☐
Expectation of workers too high	☐	☐
Other: _____	☐	☐

What did you like most about your job?

What did you like least about your job?

Did you feel we trained you properly for your current position?

Did we offer you opportunity for advancement?

Was your last supervisor fair and reasonable in their expectations?
Do you feel your contributions were appreciated by?
Your supervisor
The organization
Your co-workers
Did you have the necessary equipment to perform your job?
Were you satisfied with the overall benefit program provided? If not, what should we have offered?
What suggestions do you have for improvements?
Are there changes we could have made to maintain your relationship with us?
Who may we thank for making your time with us a positive one?
Would you like to be considered for employment with us again if an opportunity should arise?
Other comments?

Unemployment Expense Calculation

Unemployment expense is a concern for a business. Businesses often fail to realize that unemployment is like any insurance product. Your premiums are and the state (the carrier in this case) makes the payments to the unemployed. The business is only responsible for a small amount paid per employee as an insurance premium. As such, the cost to a business for a proper termination is not a financial impact that should be part of the equation for deciding whether or not to terminate.

Unemployment insurance differs greatly from one state to another. The chart below provides information about unemployment and how to calculate the rate for your state, and specifically your employee population. The cap can be found for your State on google.

Evaluate your current unemployment rate. You can find this number by looking at the tax rate in your payroll system. You will also need to determine the wage cap that is used in your state for unemployment fees. Each state sets their own rate, but only taxes up to an annual amount that minimizes the total tax due.

If you have a great deal of turnover, your unemployment fees will increase as you have more people each year who work for you and are within the payable amount. Likely, you will have to pay unemployment taxes on some employees that do not stay with your company all year and contribute to your high unemployment. For this reason, we ask you to look at the total W2's issued last year for analysis.

First, determine these two figures:

Current Rate: _____   Maximum wage cap: _____

Use this formula to review the impact unemployment has on your operation:

(current rate) X (wage cap) X (total number of W2's last year): _____

This is your typical exposure for unemployment each year. However, if you have a large part time population, you may never hit the cap for employees. In that case, enter the average wage of part time employees rather than the maximum.

Fighting unemployment claims is a frustrating and time-consuming activity. Consider the impact if you can reduce your rate by even 1%. If it is a significant number to your organization, we encourage you to engage the activities below. If the number is not a driver in your operation, then unemployment may not be worth a great deal of attention.

To reduce unemployment expense, consider these actions:

✓ Improved hiring

✓ Know the amount of time your state allows you to "test" an employee. This IS NOT your introductory period in your handbook. Many states will allow a period of time you can separate an employee and not be responsible for the unemployment

✓ Document the issues with performance and have employee sign notices of poor performance

✓ Provide a suspension without pay prior to termination

Employee Turnover Calculator

Type of Cost	Description of Cost	Cost in $
Separation Costs	Cost of exit interviewer's time	
	Cost of terminating employee's time	
	Cost of admin functions related to termination	
	Separation pay	
	Increase in unemployment tax	
	Repeated maximum of social security tax	
	Communication to team and vendors	
Replacement Costs	Cost of attracting applicants	
	Pre-employment administrative expenses (rewrite job descriptions, place job ads etc.)	
	Cost of entrance interviews	
	Testing costs	
	Staffing costs--HR and Manager	
	Travel and moving expenses	
	Post-employment info gathering and orientation (policy and procedures, wage, benefits)	
	Cost of medical exams, background checks, credit checks	
Training Costs (new hire)	Cost of informational literature (brochures, manuals)	
	Formal training costs	
	Informal training costs (On Job Training, mentoring)	
	Productivity loss (supervisor and employee)	
Performance Differential	Differential in performance cost/benefits (salary differential, vacancy lag, learning curve)	
	Overtime cost	
	Increased paid time off	
	Intangible (loss of knowledge, disruption, demoralization, stress)	
Total Turnover Costs Per Employee		

Action items for employee alignment and engagement

1.	Consider a performance alignment program that has frequent feedback

2.	Review your performance review forms – are they forward focused?

3.	Identify your top talent?

a.	Meet to insure interest and alignment?

b.	Plan to develop employee skills to meet your needs 3-5 years from now?

c.	Create budget for training and development

4.	What are your plans for creating an engaged employee community in the next 6 months?

5.	Calculate your unemployment rate and determine impact of long term expense

Employers of all sizes struggle with establishing a compensation program that is fair to employees and sustainable for the organization. There are many components of compensation that include base pay, annual increases, merit increases, and bonuses. In a smaller business, these can be overwhelming to consider. We often find it is the squeaky wheel that gets the increase in pay, because the owner or manager just didn't want to deal with it. However, this is hardly a method of rewarding employees productively and will not sustain the culture of top talent and retention we've been talking about.

Setting the proper rate for a starting salary is often based on inaccurate data, or deciding to meet the expectations of the candidate you want to hire. Employees have come to expect annual salary increases; even where productivity has not improved and new skills have not been added. Both these practices add to the long-term issues of compensation spiraling out of control. There should be a systematic way for all businesses to evaluate pay and ensure that the total rewards provided to employees are aligned with the benefits the business receives from the employee's effort.

Benefit programs offered by a company are a combination of those mandated by the government and voluntary programs. An organization has the obligation to provide Social Security, Medicare, Unemployment Insurance, and Workers' Compensation to all employees. Whether health insurance is mandatory is dependent on the size of your business today, and may change in the future. Stay tuned for that one!

How do you stay on top of the constant changes in HR?

Be sure to check out the weekly HR Topics blog!

If it's not showing up in your inbox every week, go to:

hrtopics.com to subscribe!

Total compensation is the compilation of all pay and benefits offered to employees. The focus of HR today is on total compensation, not simply the hourly or annual salary offered to employees. Employees expect paid time off for vacations, illness, bereavement, jury duty, and a myriad of other benefits that do not drive value to your bottom line. In addition, you likely provide many other benefits that are not quantified but valuable to employees such as employee discounts on products, flexible work hours, and the ability to work from a remote location. Employees need to appreciate the full value of what they receive beyond the paycheck.

Where to Find Information on Pay Rates

So how do you know if you are offering everything you should? There are some easy to access websites that will provide data on salary and benefits. Two we recommend are:

Salary.com – a comprehensive site that has data by zip code, allowing you to access information for your specific area. The site does derive its data from the employee, so for many compensation experts, it is not considered to be reliable. However, there are three reasons that it continues to be a resource for the small businessperson.

1) While self-reported, the ranges shown for positions are within close proximity of the salaries reported in more formal (and expensive) salary surveys.

2) This is where employees and candidates are looking to validate their pay. Don't you want to know what they are looking at, and can have a conversation with them about why their pay may differ from what they see on this, or other publicly available web sites?

3) It's free – virtually any way! To get more extensive data they offer a paid service, but the free information is all that is needed to get an idea of what an employee or candidate should be paid.

O*net Online (onetonline.org) – This is a service provided by the US Department of Labor which has compiled a great deal of data regarding occupations in the United States. The site is continually maintained and updated which allows you to access real time data collected by the Department of Labor. You can use O*net for:

- developing effective job descriptions
- define employee and/or job-specific success factors
- align organizational development with workplace needs
- refine recruitment and training goal
- design competitive compensation systems

The system is completely free, and used by candidates, employees and employers alike. They have recently updated the portal and it is easy to use and provides a wealth of information.

In addition to these publicly available sites, be sure you contact your specific industry association for compensation and benefit data. They should have an annual survey that you can purchase, utilize or have access to as part of the membership package. Often they will ask for participation in the survey to receive the results at a reduced fee. If so, this is time well spent.

Paying Employees Properly

The law governing pay is the Fair Labor Standards Act (FLSA) and it is essential that a member of your team is well versed in its requirements. The Fair Labor Standards Act is a complex body of regulations by the Department of Labor governing most aspects of pay including rules regarding:

- Travel pay
- Who is entitled to overtime
- Child labor
- What hours are considered work
- Employees who receive tips
- On call employees

. . . . Just to name a few!

The chart on the next page will help confirm your complete knowledge of FLSA.

Fair Labor Standards Act

FLSA is a comprehensive law that dictates how we pay employees. All businesses that have over $500,000 in sales or have Interstate operations are obligated to comply with all provisions of the act. Essentially all businesses must comply.

The table below is intended for you to verify compliance within your operation. These are the components of the fair labor standards act that impact employers on a regular basis. There are additional requirements that involve special circumstances you may want to be familiar with. Check your practices as well as any written policy you may have to ensure compliance.

	Facts about this component	Indicate whether you are complying, need training or a new policy
Minimum Wage	Minimum hourly wage to be paid to most employees. Exceptions exist for children and tipped employees. *VERIFY STATE LAW.*	
Overtime	OT must be paid 1.5 times the base wage for hours **WORKED** over 40 unless they are deemed to be exempt from the law. There are 5 specific exemption categories and a few special cases where an employee may be exempt. We have attached the Department of Labor guidance on the following pages. Some state law differs, so be aware of your regulations.	
Meals and Breaks	There is no federal law. Typically dictated by state law – ensure you are complying. If no state law, there is no requirement for most businesses.	
Definition of Hours	Businesses are required to define a pay week stating the day and time of week it begins and ends. This must be stable for a regular period, but can be any 7 consecutive days that applies to your business.	
Child Labor	Specific hours of work for those under 16 years of age. Under 18 cannot work in hazardous occupations.	
Waiting Time	If an employee is at work but unable to perform their function due to no fault of their own, they are typically due pay for that time. This may occur during equipment failure, power outage, weather etc. If the employee is sent home or given time to do as they please for any amount of time, they would typically not be due pay.	
Tipped Employees	A lower minimum wage is acceptable, but the business must ensure that base compensation plus tips for the day are at least minimum wage for hours worked.	
On call/Call Back	Employees only need to be paid for the time they are actually working – unless the on-call requirements are so restrictive they limit personal activities during the time they are off.	
Comp Time	Trading overtime worked for time off in the future. This is not currently allowed by the FLSA except for public employees.	

IT IS ESSENTIAL THAT YOU ALSO REVIEW STATE LAW, THIS OVERVIEW IS PROVIDED WITH THE FLSA IN MIND WHICH IS A FEDERAL STATUE. THE INFORMATION IN THIS CHART IS NOT COMPREHENSIVE AND ALL QUESTIONS OR VERIFICATION SHOULD BE DIRECTED TO LEGAL COUNSEL.

Additional Components to the Fair Labor Standards Act

The FLSA and Department of Labor have specific record keeping requirements. You will find this retained by most payroll systems. It is wise to check your process to ensure that each piece of information listed is retained.

1.   personal information, including employee's name, home address, occupation, sex, and birth date if under 19 years of age

2.   hour and day when workweek begins

3.   total hours worked each workday and each workweek

4.   total daily or weekly straight-time earnings

5.   regular hourly pay rate for any week when overtime is worked

6.   total overtime pay for the workweek

Salaried employees – the definition of who is entitled to overtime and how that must be paid is very strict. Whether an employee is paid on a fixed salary basis has no impact on compliance with the Fair Labor Standards Act. The only relevant point is whether an employee is subject to overtime. Only employees that are considered exempt from overtime are eligible to forgo pay for time spent over 40 hours per week. The only categories of exempt employees are:

- Executives/Managers
- Administrators
- Professionals; Learned or Creative
- Computer system professionals
- Outside Sales people

The next few pages provide details regarding each of these exemptions provided by the Department of Labor. Be aware that the exempt status follows the position, not the qualifications of the person in the position.

For example, you may have an accounts receivable clerk who is a trained accountant, but the job does not require that level of training, therefore the position is non-exempt.

Fact Sheet #17A: Exemption for Executive, Administrative, Professional, Computer & Outside Sales Employees Under the Fair Labor Standards Act (FLSA)

This fact sheet provides general information on the exemption from minimum wage and overtime pay provided by Section 13(a)(1) of the FLSA as defined by Regulations, 29 C.F.R. Part 541.

The FLSA requires that most employees in the United States be paid at least the federal minimum wage for all hours worked and overtime pay at not less than time and one-half the regular rate of pay for all hours worked over 40 hours in a workweek.

However, Section 13(a)(1) of the FLSA provides an exemption from both minimum wage and overtime pay for employees employed as bona fide executive, administrative, professional and outside sales employees. Section 13(a)(1) and Section 13(a)(17) also exempt certain computer employees. To qualify for exemption, employees generally must meet certain tests regarding their job duties and be paid on a salary basis at not less than $684* per week. Employers may use nondiscretionary bonuses and incentive payments (including commissions) paid on an annual or more frequent basis, to satisfy up to 10 percent of the standard salary level. Job titles do not determine exempt status. In order for an exemption to apply, an employee's specific job duties and salary must meet all the requirements of the Department's regulations.

See other fact sheets in this series for more information on the exemptions for executive, administrative, professional, computer and outside sales employees, and for more information on the salary basis requirement.

Executive Exemption

To qualify for the executive employee exemption, all of the following tests must be met:

- The employee must be compensated on a salary basis (as defined in the regulations) at a rate not less than $684* per week;

- The employee's primary duty must be managing the enterprise, or managing a customarily recognized department or subdivision of the enterprise;

- The employee must customarily and regularly direct the work of at least two or more other full-time employees or their equivalent; and

- The employee must have the authority to hire or fire other employees, or the employee's suggestions and recommendations as to the hiring, firing, advancement, promotion or any other change of status of other employees must be given particular weight.

Administrative Exemptions

To qualify for the administrative employee exemption, all of the following tests must be met:

- The employee must be compensated on a salary or fee basis (as defined in the regulations) at a rate not less than $684* per week;

- The employee's primary duty must be the performance of office or non-manual work directly related to the management or general business operations of the employer or the employer's customers; and

- The employee's primary duty includes the exercise of discretion and independent judgment with respect to matters of significance.

Professional Exemption

To qualify for the **learned professional** employee exemption, all of the following tests must be met:

- The employee must be compensated on a salary or fee basis (as defined in the regulations) at a rate not less than $684* per week;
- The employee's primary duty must be the performance of work requiring advanced knowledge, defined as work which is predominantly intellectual in character and which includes work requiring the consistent exercise of discretion and judgment;
- The advanced knowledge must be in a field of science or learning; and
- The advanced knowledge must be customarily acquired by a prolonged course of specialized intellectual instruction.

To qualify for the **creative professional** employee exemption, all of the following tests must be met:

- The employee must be compensated on a salary or fee basis (as defined in the regulations) at a rate not less than $684* per week;
- The employee's primary duty must be the performance of work requiring invention, imagination, originality or talent in a recognized field of artistic or creative endeavor.

Computer Employee Exemption

To qualify for the computer employee exemption, the following tests must be met:

- The employee must be compensated either on a salary or fee basis (as defined in the regulations) at a rate not less than $684* per week or, if compensated on an hourly basis, at a rate not less than $27.63 an hour;
- The employee must be employed as a computer systems analyst, computer programmer, software engineer or other similarly skilled worker in the computer field performing the duties described below;
- The employee's primary duty must consist of:
    1) The application of systems analysis techniques and procedures, including consulting with users, to determine hardware, software or system functional specifications;
    2) The design, development, documentation, analysis, creation, testing or modification of computer systems or programs, including prototypes, based on and related to user or system design specifications;
    3) The design, documentation, testing, creation or modification of computer programs related to machine operating systems; or
    4) A combination of the aforementioned duties, the performance of which requires the same level of skills.

Outside Sales Exemption

To qualify for the outside sales employee exemption, all of the following tests must be met:

- The employee's primary duty must be making sales (as defined in the FLSA), or obtaining orders or contracts for services or for the use of facilities for which a consideration will be paid by the client or customer; and
- The employee must be customarily and regularly engaged away from the employer's place or places of business.

Highly Compensated Employees

Highly compensated employees performing office or non-manual work and paid total annual compensation of $107,432 or more (which must include at least $684* per week paid on a salary or fee basis) are exempt from the FLSA if they customarily and regularly perform at least one of the duties of an exempt executive, administrative or professional employee identified in the standard tests for exemption.

Blue-Collar Workers

The exemptions provided by FLSA Section 13(a)(1) apply only to "white-collar" employees who meet the salary and duties tests set forth in the Part 541 regulations. The exemptions do not apply to manual laborers or other "blue-collar" workers who perform work involving repetitive operations with their hands, physical skill and energy. FLSA-covered, non-management employees in production, maintenance, construction and similar occupations such as carpenters, electricians, mechanics, plumbers, iron workers, craftsmen, operating engineers, longshoremen, construction workers and laborers are entitled to minimum wage and overtime premium pay under the FLSA, and are not exempt under the Part 541 regulations no matter how highly paid they might be.

Police, Fire Fighters, Paramedics & Other First Responders

The exemptions also do not apply to police officers, detectives, deputy sheriffs, state troopers, highway patrol officers, investigators, inspectors, correctional officers, parole or probation officers, park rangers, fire fighters, paramedics, emergency medical technicians, ambulance personnel, rescue workers, hazardous materials workers and similar employees, regardless of rank or pay level, who perform work such as preventing, controlling or extinguishing fires of any type; rescuing fire, crime or accident victims; preventing or detecting crimes; conducting investigations or inspections for violations of law; performing surveillance; pursuing, restraining and apprehending suspects; detaining or supervising suspected and convicted criminals, including those on probation or parole; interviewing witnesses; interrogating and fingerprinting suspects; preparing investigative reports; or other similar work.

Other Laws & Collective Bargaining Agreements

The FLSA provides minimum standards that may be exceeded, but cannot be waived or reduced. Employers must comply, for example, with any Federal, State or municipal laws, regulations or ordinances establishing a higher minimum wage or lower maximum workweek than those established under the FLSA. Similarly, employers may, on their own initiative or under a collective bargaining agreement, provide a higher wage, shorter workweek, or higher overtime premium than provided under the FLSA. While collective bargaining agreements cannot waive or reduce FLSA protections, nothing in the FLSA or the Part 541 regulation relieves employers from their contractual obligations under such bargaining agreements.

Essential Functions of a Job – Determining the essential functions of a position

Once you have reviewed the requirements, practice the exercise below. This will help you think through positions in your organization that may or may not be exempt. There will be positions in your organization that fall into a gray area of exempt or non-exempt. Consider reviewing those job descriptions with your corporate or employment attorney.

As an example, we show four tasks for an administrative assistant. You should replace those with the essential functions of the position you are evaluating. After completing the form, look at the significance, independence and other criteria to make your determination.

Describe the position:

An Administrative Assistant to the President of a large Multi-National Company

	Functions to be accomplished in position			
	Answer phone and correspondence	Greet guests and hang up coats	Get coffee and snacks	Secure travel arrangements and make changes via Internet
Was the job created with this function in mind				
Amount of time spent on function per week				
Minimum Qualifications			-	
Skills or training required				
Are the qualifications and skills enforced?				
Equipment that must be used				
Can others do this function as required?				
If the activity was eliminated, would the job be significantly altered?				
What are the consequences if this part of the job is not completed?				
Do other employees in similar jobs perform this function?				

Independent Contractors

The definition of a worker who is classified as an independent contractor is clearly defined by the Internal Revenue Service. The business and worker cannot make an agreement, unless it meets the requirements of the IRS. There must be a clear definition that the contractor is performing the work with clear autonomy on the project or function.

The criteria that the IRS considers to be relevant are the behavior, financial and type of relationship between the two entities. Any consultants hired that clearly have their own business and operate as such will likely be an independent contractor you are engaging. You must be mindful with those that may be operating as a sole proprietor to be certain they are an independent contractor rather than a part time or temporary employee.

If you utilize independent contractors on a regular basis, be certain you are up to date on the IRS requirements and your attorney agrees the contractor is in fact independent.

Some things that can be considered when determining if an independent contractor relationship exists:

_____ Did they network or advertise to find your organization?

_____ Do they provide services for other organizations throughout the year?

_____ Is there an option to work from your office or location of their choosing?

_____ Does the worker have flexibility to use their own systems and processes?

_____ Are supplies provided by the worker or your organization?

_____ Are they providing you a monthly invoice with all fees and expenses detailed?

_____ Is a written contract provided by the contractor?

_____ Do you provide a 1099 at year end?

Positive answers to these questions do not guarantee the contractor relationship, but will guide toward the type of behaviors that speak to a contractor. You must look at the full scope of the assignment and the independence of the person performing the work.

The best recommendation if there is any question is to consult the IRS web site. They have several tools to help you determine if a particular position could be classified as a contractor.

Travel Authorization Request

Business travel can be a perk for employees but can become expensive quickly. It is critical to define the level of accommodations, meals and out of pocket expenses that will be reimbursed. The form covers most situations that arise and still give employees latitude to make their own choices.

Is travel related to a client?   ☐ Yes   ☐ No

if yes, which client _____

Date of travel:		Date Submitted (DD/MM/YYYY):	
Name of Traveler:			
Purpose of Travel:			

Conditions of travel:

1. Authorization must be requested at least 21 days prior to departure.

2. Changes to a travel request must be requested within booking change allowance period. If change occurs during travel, email your manager and the office manager immediately.

3. Only travel is the pre-approved will be reimbursed.

4. Air travel will be booked in Coach/Economy for any trips shorter than 3 hours. Business class seats may be considered for longer trips.

5. Hotels will be booked in a modest, 4-star hotel. Chains such as Hilton, Hyatt and Marriott are the expected level of hotel. If you are travelling for a conference, stay at the conference hotel using the conference rate. Any hotel over $275 per night must include a detailed explanation of expense.

6. Meals will be covered at a reasonable amount for trip including travel days. Verify reasonable amount at: https://www.gsa.gov/travel/plan-book/per-diem-rates

7. Date modifications of issued tickets should only be incurred in urgent situations and must be approved in advance.

8. Travel expenses incurred on personal card or cash must be claimed within 10 days after completion of travel, otherwise the claim shall be void.

Itinerary And Dates Requested – include ground transportation as well					
Date/Time:	From:	To:	Type of Travel		
			Air	Car	Train
			Air	Car	Train
			Air	Car	Train
Hotel Reservation:			Hotel:		

Anticipated Expenses	
Air:	
Hotel:	*Include all nights and taxes*
Meals:	
Ground Transportation:	
Total expense requested	Number of days out of office:

Approvals	
Approved by:	Bill to:
Vacation time ☐ Yes ☐ No	
Additional comments:	

Benefits

Employees today appreciate a range of flexibility, convenience and self-development that may not be considered typical benefits – but they are. Often these are the components that keep employees aligned with your organization when they could be working at another organization for a higher salary. Be flexible and listen to what employees are asking for – then do your best to provide them.

Benefit-based compensation is changing quickly and will likely continue to evolve as legal requirements dictate what an employer must, or is no longer obligated, to provide. As a small business, you need to be competitive, yet may not have the resources to offer the large packages of your competitors. Consider "out of the box" ideas and be sure to promote them to your team.

Here are some ideas that may not cost a great deal, but will be meaningful to employees:

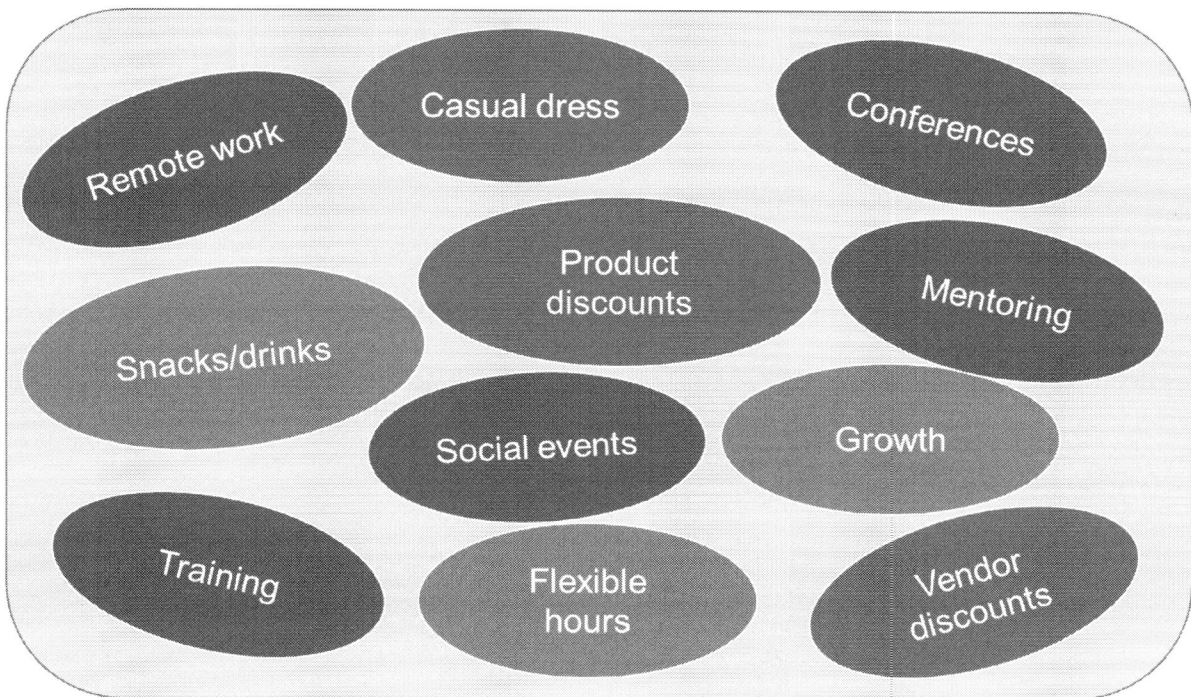

This list is not exhaustive. Speak with others in your field, connect with business people in your community – and most importantly, ask your employees. Knowing what your employees are excited about will help you provide benefits that drive results.

Total Compensation Package

The component that is often missing from a total compensation philosophy is communication. Employees tend to look at their take home pay and think of that as their compensation. Often, they forget their gross pay, and the deduction for taxes and optional benefits.. Employees need to consider their gross pay, as well as the statutory contributions being made on their behalf, as their true total compensation.

When reviewing total compensation, the numbers grow quickly. Take the base pay you consider for your employees, then add the cost of all the benefit programs provided by the organization. You will find a total compensation number is generally 30 – 45% higher than base pay. This is not an additional cost to your business; it is truly a reflection of what you are likely spending.

Consider creating a document for your employees that will visually communicate the total package you are providing in exchange for their hard work and dedication to the business. The overview can be a one-page statement of the total compensation package. Many payroll companies offer basic statements as part of the service for processing payroll. Check with your insurance broker as well. Benefit consultants will often create the statement as part of the communication of your annual program.

If you can't find a vendor to include a statement in their service offering, take the time to create it yourself. The value of an employee's total compensation package, and their lack of understanding of what you provide for them is eye opening. The statement can be completed using data from your payroll system and setting up a mail merge in Microsoft Word.

On the page that follows, you will find a sample template. This will need to be customized for your organization, but will provide a starting point if you intend to create the statements. The idea is to use the document as an overall communication tool to show employees their total compensation package. It was originally set up in Word, with the data being populated from an Excel spreadsheet.

YOUR WAGE & BENEFIT STATEMENT

Showing your
202X Total Compensation Summary

Wage & Benefit Statement prepared especially for:

INSERT EMPLOYEE NAME

Compensation Type	Company Contribution	Compensation Type	Company Contribution
Gross Wages:		Benefit Plans:	
Includes:		*Includes:*	
• Regular............................	_____	• Medical, Dental & Vision	_____
• Overtime..........................	_____	• Life & Disability.......................	_____
• Bonus	_____	• HSA contribution	_____
Employer contributions:		Social Security:	_____
20XX Stock:	_____	Medicare:	_____
401 (k) Match:	_____	Unemployment:..........................	_____
		Workers Compensation	_____

Your Total Compensation for 202X was: _____

In addition to the Compensation, you were paid for **XX** hours this year that you were off work. This equates to **$$$$** as an additional benefit.

Action Items for compensation and benefits in your organization:

1.	Understand the Fair Labor Standards Act and insure compliance

2.	Evaluate resources for market comparison of employee pay

3.	Consider adding or highlighting out of the box benefit ideas

4.	Provide total compensation statements to all employees

Chapter 7 — Technology

Human resources have seen similar advances in the use of technology as the rest of the business world. At the same time, we find a large group of HR people stuck in the past. They prefer to manage paper and don't trust employees with data entry. This just doesn't work anymore if you want to move your HR function to the top of the pyramid we showed in Chapter 1. Technology should be embraced in the human resources function as we count on computers to handle the clear majority of the administration for employee transactions.

While there may be a capital investment, keep in mind that technology doesn't get sick, and your data capture will be a higher quality than having entry-level employees input the information by hand.

In most organizations, technology should be used for:

- Processing payroll
- Allowing employees to view payroll data
- Providing data entry for employees to update personal information
- Maintaining employee files
- Administering benefits
- Tracking employee goals and performance
- Applicant tracking
- Retaining attendance information
- Employee feedback
- Communication among teams and the whole organization

Incorporating technology into your organization may run the spectrum from using Excel spreadsheets to robust human resources information systems. The ability to maintain programs and data "in the cloud" make the implementation of human resource software as simple as turning on a switch. There are many apps that will keep employees connected to your business and each other today. Apps that reside on the employees smart phone are affordable and generally require no up front cost or long term commitment.

The world of technology compliance is evolving in all aspects of business. As technology impacts human resources, critical compliance issues surround the ownership and privacy of data. Consider the chart on the next page for common issues at the intersection of employment and technology.

Technology and Employees

	Issue	Actions
Internet access	Employees are regularly given access to the Internet. The company should monitor this access and have a written policy that covers sharing of data and downloading programs onto company systems.	Consider restricting sites that are not appropriate during work hours such as job search, adult content and other sites that do not align with your culture. Train on phishing and other security issues.
Communication	Employees should be notified if their email and Internet use will be tracked and/or viewed by the company during transmission, stored or accessed in the future. Consider policies on personal communication employees have using your system.	Include this policy in the employee handbook or a separate information technology policy.
Bring Your Own Device (BYOD)	Employees commonly use their own devices to connect to organizational resources. Organizations are creating, defining, and implementing BYOD policies to address common issues with access, ownership and technology security.	Consider what you will allow or provide. Reimbursement may be required if employees use personal equipment for business purposes.
Security	It is essential to have password protection on programs, but employees typically find the need to retain passwords cumbersome. Their solution is often to have a list of passwords pinned to the cubicle wall and easily accessible to others. During employee paid time off or separation the company will need access to various systems. Look into password saving programs that can simplify the process.	How should passwords be stored and shared in your organization? How will you gain access to resources if an employee terminates without providing passwords for key programs?
Social media	An employer should not restrict an employee voicing their opinion about work. Employees must be given freedom to gather, even if that means via social media in many cases. It is OK to require employees to be clear about personal opinions stated on social media. Use caution with any restrictions on what employees can discuss with others.	Be familiar with the recommendation of the National Labor Relations Board and adopt a similar policy. This area of compliance continues to evolve and should be watched closely.

HR Technology Solutions

Implementing technology within the HR function does not have to be costly. Many of the vendors that you utilize today have solutions incorporated into their human resources products. Businesses of all sizes generally utilize an outside payroll processing vendor, and many have relationships with benefit consultants who provide Human Resources technology platforms with their services.

Have meetings with your vendors to ensure you are utilizing all that is available within their product or platform. Often there are components to the product that are included in your agreement which you may have forgotten about. Where there is an additional cost, it is generally offset by the efficiencies of quicker and more accurate processing.

Spreadsheets are often used for activities such as tracking time off and performance review dates. A little bit of training can help your administrative team create spreadsheets that can manage HR activities. The simplest of spreadsheets can be sorted by month, allowing your team to quickly know who needs what follow up during a given month. Pivot tables in spreadsheets are easy to use and will create quick tables with data that are easy to update.

There are very cost-effective programs available that will track FMLA, complete OSHA forms, calculate hours worked and more. Systems can be reviewed with confidence by visiting the Society for Human Resource Management bookstore for available options, and many are available on Amazon. There are many other resources available on the Internet at a price point that is affordable for even the smallest of businesses.

Eliminating data entry for new employees

Applicant tracking, and payroll systems allow demographic information to be entered by a candidate. This includes all the information on an application or resume that is typically re-entered by an HR or payroll person once the candidate is hired. With an integrated system, at the time a candidate is selected, HR indicates they are now an employee and the demographic information is transferred to the new employee record. The HR administrator then adds the additional relevant information such as job title, salary and hire date to the record.

Most systems will then send the new hire all paperwork necessary for their first day. Using the same technology, the new hire can complete necessary I-9, tax and banking forms to be automatically populated in your systems.

As a rule of thumb, the administrative function of the HR position accounts for approximately 50 percent of the total work completed. Proper utilization of technology will minimize this to approximately 30 percent of an HR employee's time. Technology will allow you to free up 20 percent of their day for more meaningful work.

Vendor Management

As you move toward technology which will likely include external resources, you must be sure your vendors are providing what they commit to. Today's perfect match for your needs may be an expensive or outdated resource in the future. To ensure your vendors continue to meet the needs of your organization in a cost-effective way, utilize these four steps as a regular management practice.

1) Understand capabilities

What can they do as part of the agreement
What are optional services
How will you be involved
What can't they do

2) Set expectations

What is to be delivered
Timeframes for delivery
Support and commitments needed
Acceptable quality standards
How issues will be resolved when they exist

3) Annual meeting

Meet with each vendor once a year
Review agreement
Look for items you no longer need
Ask for new features that might help you
Discuss any issues with service, personnel or
    pricing

4) Review competition every 3 years

Competition evolves as does your need, are you
    aligned with your vendor today
What might you hear from competition that your
    current vendor could provide if asked
Is the pricing you have negotiated still competitive
    in the market

Action Items for technology in your organization:

1.	**Review all manual processing of information and add technology where appropriate**
2.	**Analyze technology available from current and competitive vendors**
3.	**Update/create all policies to include Internet, Email, Social Media and BYOD**
4.	**Meet with vendors and review steps of vendor management process**

Chapter 8 — Outsourcing

Outsourcing is a process that will be considered time and time again in your organization. There are many ways to approach the outsourcing puzzle. When you consider outsourcing, don't look at it as an all-or-nothing proposition. You are most likely outsourcing portions of the HR puzzle today as a common business practice. There are many options when outsourcing and embracing outsourcing does not mean you should abandon the strategic component of the HR function.

It is a regular practice to outsource the management of the retirement plan and payroll processing since related issues of compliance or implementation can be very cumbersome for an organization to handle internally. Why bother with direct deposit and tax filing when it can be easily done by professionals at a fraction of the cost of doing it internally?

Benefit administration has several processes that might be offered by your benefit broker at no additional cost. Consider asking your vendors to provide a menu of the services they can provide and determine if you are best served with outsourcing an element of human resources administration. Be sure to ask your benefits consultant about COBRA processing, data transfer and HR database programs that are often provided.

Understand that outsourcing does not mean that you toss your personnel issues to another entity and walk away. The best outsourcing providers will require time and attention from your internal team. They will expect an internal conduit between the day-to-day employee activities and the vendor you have selected.

Sizes and Shapes of Outsourcing

There are several ways to outsource the HR function. You may choose to outsource the full function, or parts of the administrative activities. Whatever solution fits best with your organizational needs, you will want to ensure the decision is aligned with your overall strategy and goals. There are many types of businesses that handle outsourced human resources services. To ensure common understanding, we will provide an explanation of the various types of relationships your organization might have with a vendor.

Professional Employer Organization (PEO) --- The PEO will become the legal employer of your team. Employees will be paid under the federal employer identification number of the PEO and will be considered an employee of the PEO for official purposes. All tax filing, payroll obligations, unemployment etc. are the responsibility of the PEO. The PEO will handle the workers' compensation insurance and be responsible for all claims payment and evaluation of injury. Employees will receive all HR services and benefits from the PEO, including paychecks, new hire orientation, benefit administration etc. However, your organization will still have liability under the relationship referred to as co-employment. This means that although the employee technically works for the PEO, you have day-to-day interaction with the employees and must ensure that all employment laws are complied with.

Administrative Services Only (ASO) --- The relationship is similar to a PEO but does not have the co-employment component. An outside organization agrees to handle the administration involved with employee interactions with your organization. Employees are still paid under your corporate identity and you are responsible for all taxes and benefits. The ASO may or may not offer benefit packages depending on their structure and your requirements. Many ASO organizations are willing to administer the programs you have in place today.

Human Resource Groups – Consulting groups will take on the HR function in its entirety but leave the legal obligations of your employees with your organization. The goal is to create an HR function that will look and feel like an internal department to the employees. When outsourcing to a consulting firm, it is possible to arrange for both administrative and strategic support.

Independent Consultants – Sole proprietors are plentiful in many markets and seek the opportunity to support organizations that may not need a full-time HR professional. They will associate with your organization as if they are a part-time employee but work independently. Often, they have more than one client for whom they provide services. The independent contractor will be similar to a part time employee, but they will be responsible for their own taxes, benefits etc. Be careful if you are their only client that the relationship does not cross the line into a part time employee. You can do this by insisting that they set their own hours, bring their own tools (laptop computer, office supplies etc.) and submit an invoice rather than participate in your time keeping/payroll system.

Subject Matter Experts – There are many areas of human resources that only impact an organization on occasion. For these projects or reviews, consider hiring a subject matter expert that can provide services on a one-time basis. While they are similar to independent consultants, they will generally have deep knowledge in one area of human resources. For instance, there are experts in compensation, safety, communications that can be brought into your HR or leadership team as needed. This is a very cost-effective way to access the best of forward thinking processes without having to invest on an ongoing basis.

On the next page is a step by step process for evaluating various outsourcing relationships.

Engaging Outsourced Human Resources Services

WHO TO CALL FOR WHAT

Payroll processing including tax filing – Payroll firms and ASO's
Recruiting – HR consultants and staffing agencies
Leave of absence administration- ASO's and firms specializing in this area
HR technology – payroll or benefit vendor
Human Resources compliance – ASO's and Consultants
Employee customer service – ASO's
Employee training – HR Consultants
Full HR program – PEO's

SETTING A BUDGET

Consider the internal cost of the function
Determine expense that your organization can absorb

INITIAL RESEARCH INTO OPTIONS

Speak with trusted advisors
Search Internet for options and services
Conduct initial sales presentations

CREATE REQUEST FOR PROPOSALS

List essential requirements of the service
Determine items that would be nice to have if available
Evaluate qualifications of the vendor and their team
State expected deliverables
Consider timeline for return of proposals

REVIEW PROPOSALS

Fees clearly defined
Guarantees on the deliverables
Liability for errors
Culture fit with organziation
Confidence in ability to complete work

NEGOTIATING THE CONTRACT

Restate claims made in proposal
Who is responsible for additional fees and what expenses are permissable
Authority of contractor to act on behalf of company
Confidentiality
Warranties
Assignment of future work
Attorney review

IMPLEMENTION

Assign relationship to a valued internal team member
Set timetable for initial implementation
Prepare communication to internal team
Meet regularly during first three months to review
Review program and fees annually

Outsourcing does not have to be permanent

Your outsourcing needs will not remain stagnant. As the number of employees and sales volumes change, your HR needs will as well. There may be times when outsourcing all or part of the HR function is the perfect solution, and times when you need the function internally managed for greater control. If you plan for quick growth that you anticipate will level off in the future, align yourself with a partner that can take on the HR function for six to twelve months while you ramp up, and then bring HR in house. This is especially effective for startup organizations that do not have expertise in HR and need to keep their focus on the business at this stage of the organizational life cycle.

Outsourcing portions of HR administration is very advantageous in the areas of retirement plan management and payroll. There will be different needs as the organization changes, but that can be evaluated. The vendor you select today may not be the best fit in two years, and making a change is not as cumbersome as some executives think. While change is never easy, managing the process is possible and valuable when a new resource is identified.

You've almost arrived at the end of this book, but we still have a TON of resources to share with you!

If you haven't already – join our private membership group!

Email us at hacks@hrtopics.com, and we'll get you connected.

And don't forget about the HR Cards in the iTunes and Google play stores!

Grab your download now!

Action Items for outsourcing HR in your organization:

1.	**Evaluate current vendors and agreements**

2.	**Determine which HR activities, if any, should be outsourced**

3.	**Discuss the idea of full outsourcing with your leadership team**

4.	**Conduct two or three meetings with PEO's or ASO's to understand HR offerings and determine if they are appropriate for your operation**

Chapter 9 — Next Steps!

How you will embrace human resources in your organization can be a daunting and tedious task. We start with the issues that are of highest concern to the business owner, and provide tips and tricks to address the issues. The goal of this book is to help small and middle market business owners understand solutions that are available to embrace various aspects of human resources functionality.

Use this worksheet to make final decisions about HR and feel confident that you've covered all the bases. If you have too many areas of concern in the 3rd column, it may be time to consider a more dedicated resource focused on your human capital.

Consideration	HR Dependent	Need additional HR focus	Notes to address
HR Function	Asset to management team	Concerns keeping you up at night	
Strategic Plan	Dependent on Human Capital	Highly focused on technology or logistics of product	
Budget	HR a large expense	Minimal human capital expense versus sales	
Retaining top talent	Turnover rate acceptable	Constantly looking for new talent	
Non-HR management	Can focus on their business unit and processes	Focused on employees during business day	
Culture	People aligned with mission	Focused on customer and profit	

Every business relies on people to get their product to the customer. Whether it is through sales, research and development, production, or shipping, your people are what set you apart. The additional time spent with the HR function will be productive time focused on driving your business forward. What is the cost to the organization of buying capital equipment only to find that the local talent pool does not have the skills to utilize the functionality of the equipment you are so excited about? Your HR professional should be part of the conversation to build awareness early in the decision-making process.

Evaluate the culture of your business and bring in a person or organization that will support that growth and maintain the culture you want. Your HR resource needs to be available when the unexpected occurs, and that should be a consideration in your final evaluation of next steps in the human resources puzzle.

Issues will occur, but alignment with the right resources will provide comfort that they can be handled quickly and professionally – allowing you to get back to the business of running your business.

Lori Kleiman is a human resources speaker, author, and facilitator. Her more than 35 years of experience as a human resource professional and consultant gives her unique insight on how executives and business owners can address and strategically approach common HR topics to meet business goals.

Lori's business career started as the HR Manager and ended as the VP of Operations for K&S PhotoGraphics – a family owned business employing over 250 people in five states with sales of more than $13 Million. Lori also founded HRpartners, a boutique HR consulting firm that was acquired by Arthur J. Gallagher & Co. in 2007. After the acquisition, Lori continued with Gallagher for six years and led the firm's HR consulting practice before branching out again as an independent consultant, author, and speaker.

Lori's speaking and training programs cover a wide range of HR topics and are designed to provide critical HR updates and best practices to small businesses. As part of her offering, she runs mastermind groups for HR managers and consultants to stay connected with and add value to the HR profession. She has also served as an adjunct faculty member at Oakton Community College, Illinois Institute of Technology, and DePaul University, which allows her to share her love of HR with adult learners. She is currently on the advisory committee for the HR Management degree programs at Ashford University / Forbes School of Business & Technology.

Lori has a master's degree in human resources, is certified as a Senior Professional in Human Resources (SPHR), as well as SHRM-SCP designation, the highest designation available from the Society of Human Resources Management. She is a member of the National Speakers Association.

She lives in Naples Florida with her husband Andy and loves returning to her hometown of Chicago for a portion of the summers! Lori has three grown children who are each successful in their chosen professions.

Learn more about Lori at www.hrtopics.com.

HR Topics University

More Resources to Help You Manage Your HR Department and HR Career. Join Lori Kleiman as she addresses your HR questions in a variety of web-based programs.

HR Certification Prep

with a focus on how to answer the quesetions to pass your exam - our class is perfect for PHR, SHRM-CP, SPHR or the SHRM-SCP exam. We offer a varity of study options to fit

HR 101: Compliance in HR

Compliance is critical. This class offers a combination of live sessions each week and recorded content. 4 live weekly sessions covering recruiting, compensation, benefits

HR 201: Tips & tricks while running a HR Department

HR tasks don't have to be a mystery. Everything you need to accomplish someone has tackled before – so why not learn from others! In this session we will work together to

HR Topics Community

You're already a member of our community! Be sure to join the Facebook group and learn about the ongoing webinar series we offer through our private group.

HR Mastermind Group

Wanting to connect with other HR Departments of One? Join our 6-month group to make connections, learn from each other and have a sounding board for your latest idea. Add in Lori's content and the group will give you the peers you've always wanted!

Books by Lori Kleiman

Get the 2020 Release of **HR Hacks!** | *HR Hacks is More Than Just a Go-To HR Guide for Each Area of Human Resources!*
HR You Can Use | Fire HR Now | Taking Your SEAT at the Table
and many more.

Check out HR University for the most current programs and start dates
https://lori-kleiman.mykajabi.com/programs-books

HR Online Community Support and Apps

HR Hacks Membership Community

For most HR professionals, either managing a team or running an HR department of one, there aren't many places to turn to get the support and resources you need to manage everything on your plate.

I welcome you to join us in the **HR Hacks Membership Community** – the one HR community where you'll get the support and resources you can use immediately to overcome all of your HR challenges. With a quarterly subscription you receive access to:

- **Exclusive tools and documents** from HR Topics to help you run a **more efficient HR department**.

- **HR Topics Private Facebook Community** – A very responsive group of HR professional across the United States, where we share ideas, discuss on-going HR Issues and seek guidance from others; as well as Lori's frequent posts! Plus **LIVE chats with Lori Kleiman** to answer your most pressing questions and issues in HR.

- Access to **Two premium Webinars each month** – All the webinars approved for 1 CEU each for SHRM and HRCI, assuring you to get 6 CEUs each quarter.

- **Ongoing support** from peers and Lori Kleiman in a private community built exclusively for HR professionals. The ability to **share your own successes, tips,** and **strategies** to help support your HR peers

Learn more at https://lori-kleiman.mykajabi.com/offers/nkL2mzZE

HR Cards Mobile App

This app is so much more than a training tool for those planning on taking their HR Certification exam – it's a must for any HR professional. In just 5 minutes a day, HR Cards will help you master over 1200 HR specific terms in 9 different categories.

Available on both *iTunes* and *Google Play*.

Learn more at https://hrtopics.com/hr-cards/

Also by the author:

"HR departments cost money and spend the day telling managers what they can't do." We frequently hear this from CEOs of mid-sized firms. This was closely followed by, *"HR is a necessary evil."*

How do executives know the value that HR can bring? Should HR have a limited, administrative function--or be outsourced altogether? Should it be expected to have a transformative role? Should it add value to the top and bottom line every day?

Fire HR Now! is a **thought provoking** book for both CEO's and HR executives.

CEO's and HR executives can have a constructive two way conversation leading to decisions of where HR is best aligned in your organization. We look at the needs of the organization and the skills of your HR team. At the same time, the book encourages HR leaders to evaluate if their career aspirations can be met in the current organization. After reading the book, both the CEO and HR leader will be able to take the next step to **ensure HR is aligned with the organization**.

Here's the sad truth: **most businesses have a self-defeating approach to human resources.**

We know this--and the other HR issues they face--because of our proprietary survey of nearly 450 companies, averaging 78 employees.

Organizations with fewer than 200 employees often don't require--or can't afford--an HR professional. That means they frequently parse out pieces of the function to several people. This can get them in trouble--from a process or compliance standpoint. And that lack of HR focus always keeps HR in a transactional rather than a **transformational role**.

Executives never see the true meaning that would allow them to **reduce their expenses while doing a better job running their companies**.

HR You can Use! provides answers to the 5 issues keeping business owners up at night.

Walk a mile in Lori's shoes. Her career path has moved from entry level in her Family Business, building her own consulting company, HRpartners and then selling her business to a fortune 500 organization.

Taking your SEAT will help everyone with the aspiration to take their career to the next level to become the **S**trategic **E**xecutive who is **A**ction oriented and **T**echnologically savvy move ahead.

Using proven tips, techniques and templets, Lori supports your journey to the next step.

Life is about choices – and while the mantra maybe be to get your seat at the table, Lori is all about standing up and TAKING your SEAT

Today!

ALL TITLES AVAILABLE AT: http://WWW.HRTOPICS.COM

Made in the USA
Columbia, SC
09 July 2021

41538356R00085